THE CROWN GAMES OF ANCIENT GREECE

SPORT, CULTURE & SOCIETY

DAVID K. WIGGINS, SERIES EDITOR

OTHER TITLES IN THIS SERIES

George Dixon: The Short Life of Boxing's First Black World Champion, 1870–1908

Seattle Sports: Play, Identity, and Pursuit in the Emerald City

Twin Cities Sports: Games for All Seasons

Olimpismo: The Olympic Movement in the Making of Latin America and the Caribbean

Gridiron Gourmet: Gender and Food at the Football Tailgate

New Orleans Sports: Playing Hard in the Big Easy

Defending the American Way of Life: Sport, Culture, and the Cold War

Moving Boarders: Skateboarding and the Changing Landscape of Urban Youth Sports

LA Sports: Play, Games, and Community in the City of Angels

New York Sports: Glamour and Grit in the Empire City

Making March Madness: The Early Years of the NCAA, NIT, and College Basketball Championships, 1922–1951

San Francisco Bay Area Sports: Golden Gate Athletics, Recreation, and Community

Baltimore Sports: Stories from Charm City

Separate Games: African American Sport behind the Walls of Segregation

Philly Sports: Teams, Games, and Athletes from Rocky's Town

DC Sports: The Nation's Capital at Play

Frank Merriwell and the Fiction of All-American Boyhood: The Progressive Era Creation of the Schoolboy Sports Story

Democratic Sports: Men's and Women's College Athletics during the Great Depression

Hoop Crazy: The Lives of Clair Bee and Chip Hilton

A Spectacular Leap: Black Women Athletes in Twentieth-Century America

Sport and the Law: Historical and Cultural Intersections

Beyond C. L. R. James: Shifting Boundaries of Race and Ethnicity in Sports

The CROWN GAMES *of* ANCIENT GREECE

Archaeology, Athletes, and Heroes

DAVID LUNT

The University of Arkansas Press
Fayetteville
2022

978-1-68226-200-9 (cloth)
978-1-68226-201-6 (paperback)
978-1-61075-767-6 (e-book)

26 25 24 23 22 5 4 3 2 1

Manufactured in the United States of America

Designed by Liz Lester

∞ The paper used in this publication meets the minimum requirements of the American National Standard for Permanence of Paper for Printed Library Materials Z39.48–1984.

Library of Congress Cataloging-in-Publication Data

Names: Lunt, David James, author.
Title: The Crown Games of ancient Greece: archaeology, athletes, and heroes / David Lunt.
Description: Fayetteville: The University of Arkansas Press, 2022. | Series: Sport, Culture, and Society | Includes bibliographical references and index. | Summary: "The Crown Games offered a rare point of cultural unity amid the wide geography and fierce regional independence of the ancient world. This volume focuses on these festivals in the context of the ancient Greek world—a vast and sprawling territory that stretched from modern Spain to the Black Sea and North Africa"—Provided by publisher.
Identifiers: LCCN 2021039326 (print) | LCCN 2021039327 (ebook) | ISBN 9781682262016 (Paperback: acid-free paper) | ISBN 9781682262009 (cloth) | ISBN 9781610757676 (eBook)
Subjects: LCSH: Athletics—Greece—History—To 1500. | Sports—Greece—History—To 1500. | Sports—Anthropological aspects—Greece. | Sports—Social aspects—Greece—History. | Sports festivals—Greece.
Classification: LCC GV21 .L86 2022 (print) | LCC GV21 (ebook) | DDC 796.0938—dc23
LC record available at https://lccn.loc.gov/2021039326
LC ebook record available at https://lccn.loc.gov/2021039327

CONTENTS

SERIES EDITOR'S PREFACE

Sport is an extraordinarily important phenomenon that pervades the lives of many people and has enormous impact on society in an assortment of ways. At its most fundamental level, sport has the power to bring people great joy and to satisfy their competitive urges while allowing them to form bonds and a sense of community with others from various walks of life and diverse backgrounds and interests. Sport also makes clear, especially at the highest levels of competition, both the lengths that people will go to achieve victory and its close connections to business, education, politics, economics, religion, law, family, and other societal institutions. Moreover, sport is about identity development—how individuals and groups, irrespective of race, gender, ethnicity, or socioeconomic class, have sought to elevate their status and realize material success and social mobility.

Sport, Culture, and Society seeks to promote a greater understanding of the aforementioned issues and many others. Recognizing sport's powerful influence and ability to change people's lives in significant ways, the series focuses on topics ranging from urbanization and community development to biographies and intercollegiate athletics. It includes monographs and anthologies that are characterized by excellent scholarship, accessible to a wide audience, and interesting and thoughtful in design and interpretations. Singular features of the series are authors and editors who represent a variety of disciplinary areas and adopt different methodological approaches. The series also includes works by individuals at various stages of their careers, both sport-studies scholars of outstanding talent just beginning to make their mark on the field and more experienced scholars of sport with established reputations.

The latest book in the series, *The Crown Games of Ancient Greece* by David Lunt, provides important insights into the pattern of sport and its connection to other societal institutions in the ancient Greek world. Lunt does this through a meticulous and compelling examination of the Crown Games, a circuit of four prestigious festivals that included the Olympic Games held in honor of Zeus, the Isthmian Games held in honor of Poseidon, the Pythian Games held in honor of Apollo, and the Nemean Games held in honor of Zeus. Utilizing archaeological, literary, epigraphic, and other sources, Lunt explains in much detail the athletic competitions as well as the religious ceremonies, musical contests, dramatic performances, and ardent socializing and partying that took place at all these games. Explicit in his analysis is that the Crown Games were culturally significant in that they fostered a rare sense of unity during a period in Greek history in which individual city-states were decidedly and passionately independent. Lunt also furnishes a compelling analysis of the evolution of contest sites as sanctuaries at each of the festivals and how and why sport was so central to this development. Finally, Lunt explores the lives and careers of the great athletes who distinguished themselves in the Crown Games and became heroes among their fellow Greeks. The most famous of these athletes was the legendary Milo of Croton, who dominated wrestling in the late sixth century BCE, capturing multiple titles in the Crown Games that brought him lasting fame.

David K. Wiggins

AUTHOR'S PREFACE

The Crown Games comprised a circuit of four festivals held regularly in ancient Greece at Olympia, Delphi, Nemea, and Isthmia. These four sites, sacred to the gods, featured magnificent temples, lavish dedications, crowded festivals, and—of course—exhilarating athletic competitions. The sites and stories of the four Crown Games, and their role in ancient Greek society, are the subject of this book. It would be impractical to offer in the coming pages a comprehensive architectural and archaeological history of all four Crown Games sites. The sites are too big, the chronology too vast, the historical importance too profound, and the scholarship too profuse. However, it is possible to give here an introduction to the Crown Games sites and their buildings, shrines, temples, and athletic facilities, as well as the stories of some of the athletes who competed and won in the Crown Games. Understandably, the famous games at Olympia have received the bulk of scholarly attention, both ancient and modern, yet the other three sites have rich histories and archaeologies of their own. A comprehensive approach to all four of these sites offers a more detailed and contextualized approach to ancient Greek athletics. This book seeks to address the Crown Games as a circuit, integrating the development of the four sites into a broader context of Panhellenic competition and religious life. A synthesis of archaeology, epigraphy, myth, and historical accounts of the Crown Games offers a more complete picture of the history, development, and significance of these games in ancient Greece. Furthermore, this book will suggest that the Panhellenic sites and contests provided a common cultural touchstone for the otherwise disparate and often-truculent Greek city-states. Beyond merely separating winning and losing athletes, the sites and contests of the Crown Games provided opportunities for the Greeks to advocate for and to find common purpose.

Through an examination of literary, archaeological, epigraphic, and other kinds of ancient sources, this book seeks to address the questions: What were the Crown Games, what did they mean to the ancient Greeks, and what roles did they play in culture and society? The Crown

Games offered a vehicle for individual athletes to claim status and reputation. They allowed city-states to capitalize on their associations with the games and sanctuaries to advance their civic standing and communal pride. Finally, the Crown Games offered avenues for inter-Hellenic communication and relationships. Although the Greek city-states were independent political entities for much of the time frame treated in this book, the inhabitants of these cities shared religious, social, and cultural beliefs and practices. Nowhere in ancient Greek society are these shared customs more readily apparent than in the sites and events associated with the Panhellenic Crown Games.

The subject of ancient Greek athletics is well-trodden ground that has been carefully mapped in multiple modern books and articles, and most of these are very well done. However, no work of recent date has substantially integrated all four of the Crown Games into one treatment using archaeological, literary, art-historical, and epigraphic sources. While the athletic program at ancient Olympia has received a considerable amount of scholarly (and not-so-scholarly) attention, other sites and features of the ancient Crown Games remain mostly unexamined. For example, the Pythian Games at Delphi featured an extensive program of musical competitions, contests that today largely go unremarked in discussions of ancient athletics. The Nemean Games were relocated to Argos for hundreds of years. And the site at Isthmia featured a prominent theater that figured into the competitive context at the Isthmus of Corinth. These issues and others deserve to be integrated into the discussion of the ancient Crown Games.

This book will necessarily limit its focus to the world of the ancient Greeks in its most traditional and, perhaps, most mundane iteration. The sites of Olympia and Delphi, in particular, are vast and possess thousands of years' worth of interesting and compelling archaeological material. Neolithic settlers left traces of their presence in the Nemean valley, Bronze Age ruins lie beneath the sanctuary of Zeus at Olympia, Roman-era inscriptions adorn some of the surviving walls at Delphi, and Isthmia features the remains of a fifth-century-CE fortress built to repel a Visigoth invasion. Because of the enormity of the scope of the archaeological, historical, and cultural records of these locations, this book will generally limit itself to the Archaic (ca. 800–480 BCE), Classical (480–323 BCE), and Hellenistic (323–31 BCE) periods of Greek history, or—more specifically—roughly from 800 BCE, when the Archaic period witnessed the development of Greek political and military organization into small independent city-states (referred to as "poleis" or, in singular form, "a polis"), to the middle of the Hellenistic era in the second century BCE, when the arrival of Roman armies signaled a profound transformation in Greek culture and the balance of power in the Mediterranean world.[1]

While the Greeks of the Bronze Age and Iron Age certainly maintained a presence at some of the Crown Games sites, the dearth of literary records from these periods precludes much more than speculation about anything beyond the material remains. At the other end of our chronology, the incursion of Roman influences on the Crown Games represented, at least to my mind, a marked and profound shift from the traditional conceptual underpinnings of ancient Greek athletic competitions. Certainly, Greek games in the Roman world (and Romans in the world of the Greek games) are subjects worthy of attention, and recent years have brought welcome scholarly contributions in this field. However, ancient sources indicate that Roman attitudes toward athletics were very different from the attitudes of the ancient Greeks. Although the Romans crop up in various chapters of this book as part of the overall narrative (especially for their role at Isthmia), in general, this project leaves the Crown Games during the Roman era for a different investigation to be undertaken at a future date. For this book, the Crown Games sites during the approximately six hundred years from the Archaic period to the arrival of the Roman legions provide ample material for dissection, analysis, and understanding of these most prestigious athletic contests of the ancient Greek world.

The Sources

An old adage holds that a historian is only as good as the available sources, and this is certainly the case with respect to investigating the Crown Games of ancient Greece. Although there are some frustrating gaps in our knowledge of the religious ceremonies and athletic programs at the Crown Games sites, a vast amount of information is available, and this stems from historical, literary, epigraphic, and archaeological sources. Although this book draws from many sources, it will be useful to introduce here a few of the most commonly mentioned.

The most influential ancient literary source on the Crown Games is certainly the Roman-era travel writer Pausanias.[2] Born in the second century CE, Pausanias was a well-traveled Greek who wrote extensively of his journeys throughout Greece, although we know very little else about his life. Pausanias often included in his account of his travels transcriptions of inscriptions or poetic epigrams, anecdotes of local flavor, and larger historical and mythic narratives that corresponded to the geographic locations he was describing. Although archaeology has revealed considerable gaps in Pausanias's coverage and descriptions of various sites, he remains indispensable as a source for understanding the sites of the four Crown Games, especially the sites of Olympia and Delphi. Pausanias's main shortcoming for the purposes of our study is the late date at which he lived. His travels took place in the second century CE—around seven hundred years after the development of the Crown Games circuit. It therefore can become difficult to determine whether Pausanias was describing the games of his own time, the games of earlier eras, or some combination of the two. In addition, some of the more incredible details that he recorded suggest the embellishments of time. Perhaps recognizing the difficulties of distinguishing fact from fiction in his encounters, Pausanias himself notes that he does not always believe what he is told. In his words, "I am bound to record the Greek traditions, but I am not bound to believe them all."[3] Even with the chronological distances between modern-day readers and Pausanias and between Pausanias and the earliest days of the Crown Games, the traveler's narrative and description are vital for understanding the world of ancient Greek athletics.

Another ancient description of the Greek sanctuaries comes from Strabo, a geographer who wrote a seventeen-book study called *Geography* during the early years of the Roman Empire. Strabo's is a much more succinct account of the ancient Greek sites, and his descriptions of important places sometimes consist of only a paragraph or two, yet he offers an important second voice or source to corroborate and complement Pausanias.

Besides these deliberate descriptions of the sites and monuments of the Crown Games, numerous anecdotes, allusions, and accounts survive in the works of various ancient historians. The Classical period historians Herodotus, Thucydides, and Xenophon all describe historical figures and events in the context of the Crown Games. The writings of Plutarch, including his *Parallel Lives* and his collection of essays and tales, called *Moralia*, date from the first and second centuries of the Common Era. Plutarch wrote prolifically, and his role as a priest of Apollo at Delphi lends considerable credibility to his information about the sanctuary there and the attendant Pythian Games. Other important sources from the second and third centuries are Lucian and Philostratus. In a variety of settings, Lucian's dialogues bring to life the Greek world as it existed under Roman rule. His dialogue *Anacharsis, or Athletics* records an imagined conversation between the revered Athenian politician Solon (one of the Seven Sages of ancient Greece) and Anacharsis, a Scythian who is unfamiliar with Greek customs and culture, especially athletics. Of course, Solon is able to demonstrate to his guest the immense value of Greek athletic training and in turn offers the modern reader a glimpse of the Greek athletic ideal. Another writer of the Roman Empire, Philostratus, whose surviving works could actually be the products of more than one member of his family, wrote a book called *Gymnasticus*, a sort of history of, guide to, and praise of exercise and training. In another book, the *Life of Apollonius of Tyana*, Philostratus recounts the wanderings of a second-century-CE holy man who spent a considerable amount of time at Olympia.

In addition to the historical writers, an important source for understanding the Crown Games of ancient Greece is the victory, or epinician, poetry that commemorated the accomplishments of victorious athletes. The most renowned of the poets of this genre was Pindar, who lived and composed his poems in the Classical period during the fifth century BCE. Over forty of Pindar's poems survive, at least in parts, and they laud the virtues and achievements of various victorious athletes in all four of the Crown Games festivals. These athletes who paid Pindar's presumably pricey commissions seem to have profited from the transactions. After all, more than two thousand years later, the fame of these athletic champions continues to be published and commemorated. Other lyric poets, such as Bacchylides and Simonides, who wrote in the sixth and fifth centuries BCE, also composed epinician verses for their clients, with more modestly enduring fame and success.

Historians and poets are some of the most accessible sources for scholars of ancient Greek sport, but there are other veins of information to mine, especially those deriving from material culture. Numerous inscriptions connected to the Crown Games have been recovered from all four sites, and epigraphy offers some of the best primary-source documentation of the functioning of the sanctuaries in general, as well as information about ancient athletes and athletics. These inscriptions have been collected and published in a variety of series, usually connected to the archaeological excavations at each site. Archaeological excavations and their subsequent publication and interpretation are vital sources for understanding the development of the Crown Games over time, their religious contexts, and the material culture that accompanied them. Paintings found on pottery depicting athletes, equipment, training, and competition provide a visual record of the events. Although it survives only rarely, sculpture can offer a three-dimensional record of idealized athletes or their victory monuments.

Since this book is intended as an introduction to the sites and major themes of the Crown Games, the notes and commentary will favor ancient sources and archaeological reports to direct readers to the original information. Of course, there is a tremendous amount of relevant modern scholarship connected to many of these sites and issues, and I include some of this where appropriate. However, in accordance with this book's purpose and audience, citations of modern sources will be minimized, and the reader encouraged to consult the bibliography for additional information and resources. Unless otherwise noted, all translations are my own. I willingly confess to some inconsistency in transliterating Greek names and terms, sometimes using Latinized forms and sometimes preferring modern conventions. My guiding principle has been clarity and consistency, but I recognize that what seems clear to me may not be readily apparent to the reader. Specific sources for each of the Crown Games sites will be introduced in more detail in their respective chapters. However, first it is necessary to understand the role of athletics in ancient Greek society and to investigate what actually took place during the Crown Games.

ACKNOWLEDGMENTS

I wish to thank the many people who have helped and supported me in this project over the years as I worked to complete it. I recognize the enormous impact that my own teachers had on my research interests, particularly W. Lindsay Adams, Mark Munn, Daniel Berman, Stephen Wheeler, the late Paul Harvey, and the late Garrett Fagan. Thank you to Mark Dyreson for introducing me to the world of sport history. My academic "big brother" Timothy Howe at St. Olaf College has encouraged my work for as long as anyone. I thank my friends and colleagues at Southern Utah University (SUU) for years of friendship and collaboration. I especially appreciate my SUU colleague David Maxwell for helping me and teaching me about making maps. I am grateful to SUU's Department of History, Sociology, and Anthropology, College of Humanities and Social Sciences, and Office of the Provost for their financial support. I am grateful for the support of my former provost Bradley Cook, now president of Snow College in central Utah and still the only person I have seen run an entire mile in the stadium at Olympia. I thank Daniel Levine and the American School of Classical Studies at Athens for introducing me to Greece and Greece to me many years ago.

My longtime friends John Gleaves, Matthew Llewellyn, and Toby Rider of California State University, Fullerton, (CSUF) have graciously welcomed me into their annual study-abroad program in Greece, where we have spent many days visiting the sites and many nights discussing the meanings of the ancient Crown Games. Their friendship and encouragement have meant more to me than words can tell. I am grateful to my students at Southern Utah University and to the students at CSUF, whose relentless curiosity fuels my own.

The editorial team at the University of Arkansas Press has supported this project since its inception, and I am deeply grateful to David Wiggins for his guidance and to David Scott Cunningham for his dogged optimism and perseverance, especially during the COVID-19 pandemic. The efforts of Janet Foxman and Katie Herman's keen editorial eyes were vital components of this book's development, and I thank both of them for their tireless work on my behalf. I also thank the anonymous reviewers who helped to refine and shape this manuscript and its ideas. Of course, any errors that remain are mine alone. Thank you to Hans Goette at the Deutsches Archäologisches Institut in Berlin for permission to use his site plan of Olympia, and thank you to the American School of Classical Studies at Athens for its help and permission to use site plans of Isthmia and Nemea. I also thank the École française d'Athènes for the plan of ancient Delphi that appears in this book.

Many thanks to my family for years of love and support: my parents, Ed and Penny Lunt; my sisters, Jennifer Moore, Allison Lunt, and Amanda Kimball; and my brother, Marshal Lunt. Thank you, Jen, for being the first to read this manuscript and for being the family's best author. Finally, and most importantly, I thank the three Graces in my life: my spouse Jana Lunt and my daughters Zola Lunt and Juno Lunt. Their love is my greatest crown.

ABBREVIATIONS

AJA	*American Journal of Archaeology*
BCH	*Bulletin de correspondance hellénique*
FD	*Fouilles de Delphes*, École française d'Athènes.
CID	*Corpus des inscriptions de Delphes*. 4 vols. Paris, 1977–2002.
IAG	Luigi Moretti. *Iscrizioni agonistiche greche*. Rome, 1953.
IG	*Inscriptiones Graecae*. Berlin, 1873–.
IvO	Wilhelm Dittenberger and Karl Purgold, eds. *Die Inschriften von Olympia*. Berlin, 1896.
JHS	*Journal of Hellenic Studies*
NIO	Peter Siewert and Hans Taeuber, eds. *Neue Inschriften von Olympia*. Vienna, 2013.
PMG	D. L. Page, *Poetae Melici Graeci*. Oxford, 1962.
RA	*Revue archéologique*
SEG	*Supplementum Epigraphicum Graecum*
SIG	Wilhelm Dittenberger, ed. *Sylloge inscriptionum graecarum*. Leipzig, 1883–.
TAPA	*Transactions of the American Philological Association*
TrGF	Bruno Snell, Richard Kannicht, and S. L. Radt, eds. *Tragicorum Graecorum fragmenta*. 6 vols. Göttingen, Germany, 1971–2004.

THE CROWN GAMES OF ANCIENT GREECE

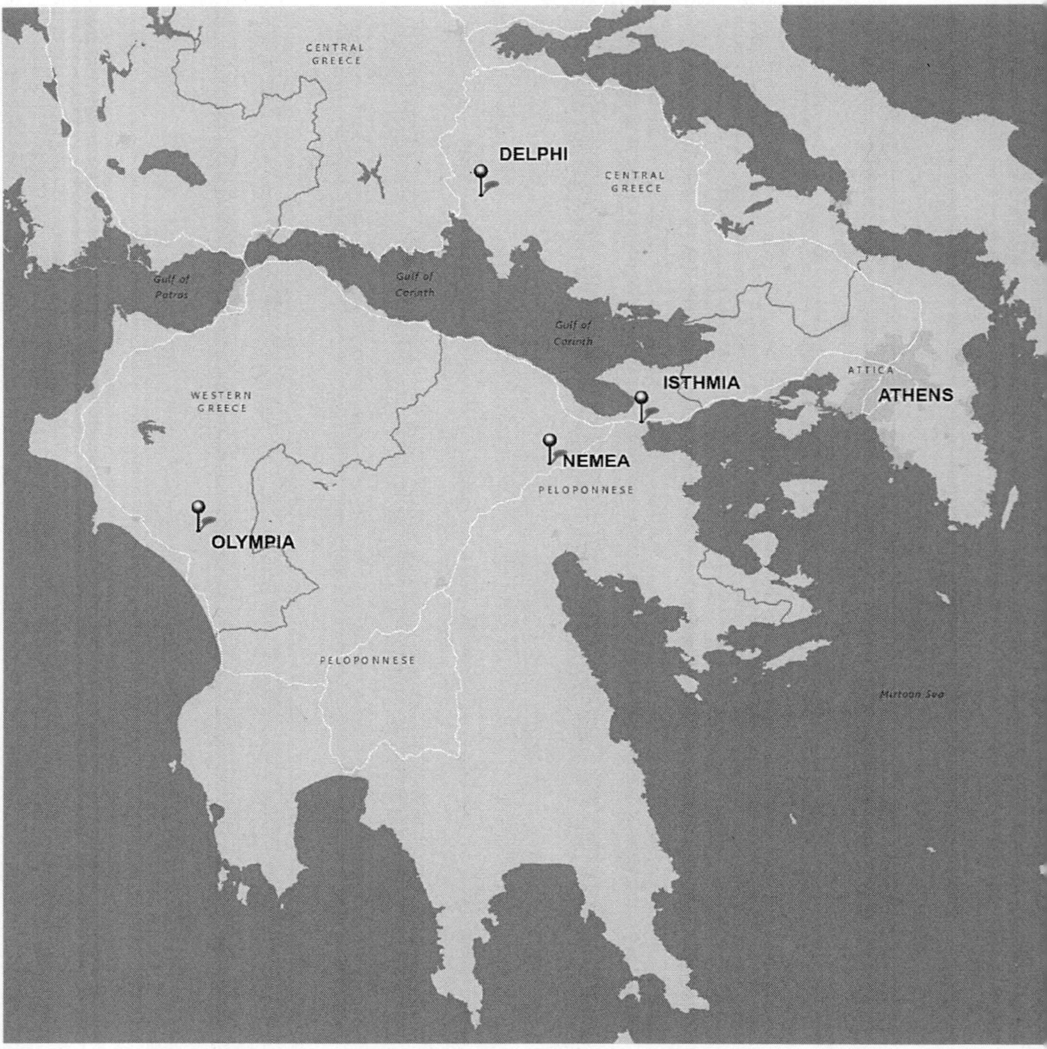

The locations of the Crown Games of ancient Greece: Olympia, Delphi, Isthmia, and Nemea. Map created using an ArcGIS Online map in conjunction with Esri software.

INTRODUCTION

Hail, glorious victor!

—Fragment of the victory song of Archilochus

Ancient Greek society was intensely competitive. Everywhere from the open-air debates of the citizen assemblies to the religious festival games, the ancient Greeks routinely attempted to best one another in endeavors such as warfare, dancing, artwork, music, comedy and tragedy, speech giving, and, of course, athletics. A typical ancient Greek male grew up participating in athletic training in his local gymnasium as part of a larger educational program. Indeed, for at least part of ancient Greek history, basic athletic training was considered an essential element of citizenship as young men trained their bodies for war and their minds for civic service. Adult men continued to use the gymnasium for its manifold purposes, including socializing, exercising, and recreation.[1] For the best athletes in town, regular community and regional festival games recognized small-time champions and offered them local bragging rights. For elite athletes, those who enjoyed dominant victories in the local and regional competitions, there were more prestigious contests, such as the Panathenaic festival at Athens, the Heraia at Argos, and the games to Apollo held on the island of Delos. Victory in these contests was lucrative and prestigious, but the greatest prize an ancient Greek could strive for was a victory in the four Crown Games held regularly at Olympia, Delphi, Isthmia, and Nemea.

The Crown Games were the apex of athletic competition. These were a circuit of competitions that took place at four locations in Greece during the course of one four-year cycle. The best known of the Crown Games took place at Olympia, and ancient historians and writers often referred to the four-year cycle of games as an Olympiad in their chronologies. The ancient Olympian Games were the most prominent and prestigious of all of the Greek contests, and the birth of the modern Olympic movement has only reinforced the unrivaled status of ancient Olympia in contemporary consciousness. However, the Crown Games included much more than the contests at Olympia: games at Delphi for Apollo, called the Pythian Games; the Isthmian Games for Poseidon; and the Nemean Games, sacred to Zeus, all enjoyed considerable prestige of their own as part of the Crown Games. Although victors in the Crown Games could expect sizeable and valuable prizes when they returned home—one ancient source claimed (perhaps anachronistically) that a sixth-century-BCE Athenian victor in the Olympian Games received a lucrative cash reward of 500 drachmas from the state—the only prize awarded at these four festivals themselves was a simple crown made of olive, pine, celery, or laurel branches and leaves, which caused ancient writers to label these prestigious contests the "Crown" Games.[2]

The ancient Greeks celebrated the Crown Games with only occasional disruptions for hundreds of years. The four festivals emerged as a regularized, organized circuit in about 580 BCE, and this circuit continued for over nine hundred years until the end of the fourth century of the Common Era. The oldest and most prestigious of the Crown Games was the Olympian festival, and the other games were arranged to complement the quadrennial Olympiad. The Pythian Games at Delphi took place at the midpoint of the Olympiad and were also celebrated once every four years. By contrast, the Isthmian and Nemean Games were held every two years, so an Olympiad cycle of four years actually included six different Crown Games—one Olympian, one Pythian, two Nemean, and two Isthmian festivals.

A typical Crown Games cycle, or *periodos*, started with the Olympian festival, held during the second full moon after the summer solstice, a date that typically fell in the late summer. The Nemean Games were held a year later, during the next summer. The Isthmian Games took place seven or eight months after those at Nemea, in the following spring, followed by the Pythian Games in the summertime, just two or three months later. Then midway through the Olympiad, one year after the Pythian Games, the ancient Greeks held another Nemean festival in the summertime. Another set of the Isthmian Games took place the following spring, before the next Olympian Games that summer and thus the beginning of a new cycle.[3] In essence, there was a Crown Games festival every summer (Olympian, Nemean, or Pythian), and the biennial Isthmian festival occurred in the springtime of the Olympian and Pythian years.

TYPICAL CROWN GAMES CYCLE,
OR *PERIODOS*

Year 0, Summer	Olympian Games
Year 1, Summer	Nemean Games
Year 2, Spring	Isthmian Games
Year 2, Summer	Pythian Games
Year 3, Summer	Nemean Games
Year 4, Spring	Isthmian Games
Year 4, Summer	Olympian Games

Note: Of course, since they lacked the number zero, ancient Greeks would have counted the years inclusively, starting at one.

The ancient Greek world was vast and sprawling, incorporating far more area than the modern nation of Greece. Ancient Greeks settled throughout the Mediterranean area, as far west as Spain and southern France and in North Africa to the south, and the Black Sea region consistently yields evidence of its ancient Greek settlers. During the Hellenistic period (beginning in 323 BCE), ancient Greeks spread even more widely, with major kingdoms developing in Ptolemaic Egypt and Seleucid Syria. With such a wide scope and a fiercely independent disposition among the Greek city-states, the Crown Games offered a rare opportunity for ancient Greeks from throughout the world to assemble in some form of cultural and religious unity.

Besides its role as a cultural touchstone, the cycle of the Crown Games occupied an important position in ancient Greek time reckoning. Since the games were Panhellenic—that is, open to all Greeks—reckoning time by Olympiads offered a consistent system in a society where many independent cities used their own calendar systems. An ancient Greek mechanical device discovered in the early twentieth century in a shipwreck off the coast of the island of Antikythera sheds some light on this practice. The Antikythera Mechanism features an intricate system of gears and inscribed wheels intended to keep track of various lunar, stellar, solar, and human cycles and calendars. Modern-day scholars and scientists working on the remains of the device have learned that, when it was intact, the device could be used to calculate time, anticipate solar and lunar eclipses, and keep a dizzying array of other chronological sequences in sync with one another. Appropriately, among its many dials is one that archaeologists and scholars have dubbed the "Games Dial," since its inscribed surface accounts for the Crown Games circuit over a span of four years.[4] In addition, several ancient historians organized their narrative chronologies by referring to Olympiads, using this common basis to organize and harmonize the events of the past.

From the 500s BCE until the 300s CE, a span of over nine hundred years, the Crown Games represented a standard of chronological continuity for the classical world, although—as we will see—the games at Isthmia and Nemea were not immune to severe disruptions. More or less, though, for these nine-plus centuries, ancient Greeks and—eventually—Romans periodically journeyed to these sanctuaries where they could walk in sacred processions, witness solemn animal sacrifices, listen to poetic performances, and, of course, enjoy watching their society's highest levels of athletic competition.

A victory in the Crown Games represented the pinnacle of athletic achievement, and the programs of athletic events grew, shrank, or otherwise changed in conjunction with the popularity of the games and the resources of the administrators. Over time, the religious sanctuaries at Olympia, Delphi (where the Pythian Games took place), Nemea, and Isthmia underwent significant modifications as buildings were raised, remodeled, or otherwise repurposed to fit the needs of the time. As the crowds increased and the sanctuaries welcomed more and more pilgrims, athletes, and fans, the administrators of these sanctuaries constructed temples and shrines and expanded the facilities for visitors and spectators. Wealthy benefactors paid for the construction of fountains and guesthouses, Greek city-states erected "treasuries" and monuments to showcase their prosperity and achievements, and victorious athletes dedicated statues of themselves to commemorate and publicize their achievements. While these religious sanctuaries underwent constant and consistent changes, improvements, and renovations, they also suffered from fires, warfare, neglect, and even abandonment at times. The vibrant, changing, and complicated nature of these sanctuaries did not go unnoticed in antiquity. Indeed, one of our best sources, the Roman-era travel writer Pausanias, dedicated nearly two of the ten books of his work to the wonders of Olympia and most of another book to the sanctuary of Apollo at Delphi, in both cases recording the development of and changes to the sanctuaries and their games over time.

The importance of the Crown Games notwithstanding, the sanctuaries that hosted these festivals spent the majority of the time operating as religious institutions. They were open to visitors year-round and hosted a small number of full-time priests and religious officials who oversaw regular sacrifices and the maintenance of the sites' buildings and facilities. In addition to the Crown Games, these sanctuaries celebrated other religious festivals and fulfilled sundry religious and civic roles and functions. For example, the sanctuary at Delphi, with its famous oracle of Apollo, was consistently choked with omen seekers and pilgrims, and ancient evidence attests to a prominent role for the god Dionysus in the sanctuary as well.[5] At Olympia, in addition to the festival to Zeus, the sanctuary hosted the Heraia, a festival dedicated to Zeus's wife and sister, Hera, that featured a limited athletic program for girls and young women. Beyond these religious observances, the Panhellenic nature of these sanctuaries offered opportune and advantageous meeting spots for Greek diplomatic assemblies.

The Panhellenic Sanctuaries

As neutral territory sacred to the gods, the sanctuaries at the Crown Games sites welcomed delegations from the often-fractious Greek world to meet, debate, and negotiate their political affairs. In an ancient Greek world torn by dissent, rivalry, and relentless competition, the sanctuaries of the Crown Games provided an important venue for Greeks to meet on common cultural and religious grounds. When it came to diplomacy, these sites offered regular opportunities for negotiation and dialogue.

At Delphi, a religious association called the Delphic Amphictyony offered a limited system of Panhellenic cooperation and dialogue. Representatives from the regions around the sanctuary met regularly to govern the affairs of the site, and the importance of Delphi lent this council significant authority in wider Greek affairs.

Delphi's importance for all of Greece was evident in the wake of the Persian Wars. In 479 BCE, after the Battle of Plataea, as the Greeks were chasing the Persians from their lands, the oracle at Delphi instructed the victorious Greeks to extinguish all of the fires that had been polluted by Persian invaders and then to rekindle them with fresh and pure fire from the public altar at Delphi. Consequently, a runner named Euchidas was sent from Plataea to Delphi. At Delphi, Euchidas was purified, crowned with laurel, and given new fire to spread to the Greeks. Euchidas, according to the ancient writer Plutarch, then ran from Delphi back to Plataea (a distance that Plutarch recorded as "a thousand stades" but that is in fact closer to a hundred kilometers) in one day, delivered the fire, and promptly collapsed and died.[6] It was Delphi, a site belonging to and connected to the gods, that provided purified fire to all of the victorious Greeks and reinforced the shared Greek identity of the soldiers and citizens who had resisted the Persian invasion.

Like Delphi, Olympia served an important Panhellenic purpose aside from its athletic festivals. An ancient inscription on a bronze plaque from Olympia dated to the fifth century BCE indicates that the site possessed some kind of inter-Hellenic court of arbitration for Greek city-states, although the specifics are poorly understood.[7] Sometime after the dramatic Athenian-led naval victory over the Persians in the Battle of Salamis in 480 BCE, the Athenian commander Themistocles attended the Olympian Games. The story goes that the Panhellenic audience preferred to watch and applaud the war hero Themistocles rather than the athletes who were competing in the stadium.[8] In 428 BCE, during the Peloponnesian War, the people of the island of Lesbos revolted from Athenian control. The Athenian historian Thucydides, an eyewitness to much of the war's action, tells how envoys from the Lesbian city of Mytilene sailed to the Greek mainland and met with the Spartans to ask for help against the Athenians. The Spartans directed the envoys from Mytilene to go to Olympia, and there at the festival, an assemblage of Spartans and their Peloponnesian allies heard the pleas for help from the people of Mytilene. Clearly, the Panhellenic sanctuary offered a valuable site for Greeks to meet and engage in diplomatic discourse under the protection of Zeus. Indeed, the Mytilenean envoys emphasized their location in their speech, asking the Spartans and their allies not to dishonor Olympian Zeus and his temple by ignoring their request for help.[9] Seven years later, in 421 BCE, when the Spartans and Athenians concluded a peace treaty, the two sides agreed that each would annually renew its oath to abide by the agreement. Accordingly, the Greeks erected pillars at the Panhellenic sites of Olympia, Delphi, and Isthmia, as well as at Sparta and Athens, to commemorate this treaty and promote the renewal of the oaths.[10]

On the other hand, the Panhellenic nature of the Crown Games festivals did not always promote harmony among the fractious city-states. In 420 BCE, for example, the Eleans, who administered the Olympian Games, barred the Spartans from the sanctuary, claiming that a Spartan military force had violated the sacred truce by seizing some land near

Olympia. Worried that the Spartans would force their way into the sanctuary to sacrifice at the Temple of Zeus, the games' overseers stationed a heavily armed group of Eleans, along with soldiers from Argos, Mantineia, and Athens, to keep watch during the festival. One Spartan entrant disguised his chariot as an entry from Thebes, but he was discovered and whipped by the judges when his chariot won and he came forward to celebrate his victory. Tensions remained high throughout the festival, but the Spartans allowed it to continue undisturbed.[11] Although the ancient source notes that the Spartans were banned from competing in the games, it was the right to sacrifice at the Temple of Zeus during the festival that the Spartans most desired, which underscores the religious importance of the ancient Olympian festival.[12] Several years later, in 412 BCE, as the Spartans and their Peloponnesian allies were readying a stealthy attempt to send warships to liberate the island of Chios from Athenian control, the Isthmian Games hindered the plan's effectiveness. The historian Thucydides reported that the Corinthians were unwilling to accompany the flotilla until the Isthmian Games had concluded. The Spartan-led fleet lost valuable time while the games went on and they waited for the Corinthians. Furthermore, Athenians in attendance at the games got wind of the plan, which allowed the Athenians time to prepare.[13] Clearly, at times, the role of the Panhellenic sites and festivals in bringing the Greek world together led to rivalries and warfare as well as to diplomacy and cultural unity.

In addition to the games serving as diplomatic gatherings of political and military leaders, ancient Greek Sophists, philosophers, orators, and speech writers took advantage of the vast and varied crowds at the festivals to showcase their abilities and their ideas. The fifth century BCE's Gorgias of Leontini, a famed Sicilian orator and sophist who made his living in Athens, offered an oration at the Olympian Games urging the Greeks to end their wars against one another and to unify against the Persians.[14] The speech writer Lysias composed a similar speech for the Olympian crowds in 388 BCE, as did the noted scholar Isocrates in around 380 BCE. All three of these intellectuals looked to the Panhellenic nature of the festival crowds in their efforts to inspire the Greeks to work together in common cause.[15] Sadly for the Greeks, the exhortations of the philosophers and Sophists failed to move them to act, and their endemic wars continued.

The opportunity to make dramatic announcements to a large and varied assemblage of Greeks from throughout the Greek-speaking world was not lost on Alexander the Great. During the Olympian festival of 324 BCE, Alexander, who was campaigning in Asia, sent instructions for the herald at the Olympian Games to read a letter to all of the assembled Greeks. Alexander's decree required all of the cities of Greece to receive back their exiled citizens, a decision that was met with shouts of approval by the reported twenty thousand exiles in attendance at the festival.[16] Alexander's decree certainly carried a political purpose, but the decision to announce his decision at the Olympian Games denotes the Panhellenic and comprehensive nature of the festival. In no other venue could a single announcement reach such a large and diverse crowd of Greeks, and the religious nature of the sanctuary presumably lent gravity to Alexander's pronouncement.

As were the sanctuaries at Olympia and Delphi, the sanctuary of Poseidon at Isthmia was a diplomatic meeting place for ancient military and political leaders. After the Battle of Salamis in 480 BCE, an assembly of Greek military commanders met at the sanctuary at Isthmia. There, at the altar of Poseidon, they each voted for the Greek who they believed had done the most to win the great victory.[17] During the Hellenistic period, the Achaean military commander Philopoemen enjoyed a moment of Panhellenic acclaim at the Nemean Games. In 207 or 206 BCE, Philopoemen had engineered a military victory for the Achaeans (the inhabitants of a region of the Peloponnesian peninsula known as Achaea) against the Spartans. At the Nemean Games in 205 BCE (which were held at Argos—a change in location that will be discussed in the chapter on Nemea), Philopoemen happened to enter the theater during a musical competition. As one of the competing performers, in the course of his song, praised the "glorious state of freedom" of the Greeks, the story goes, the assembled spectators turned to Philopoemen and applauded him, attributing to him their gratitude and hopes for their continued freedom from the Spartans.[18]

Alas, this freedom was not to last. Within a decade, much of Greece had been subdued by Roman armies under the command of Titus Quinctius Flamininus. Flamininus, however, understood the importance of the Crown Games and their Panhellenic nature. In 196 BCE, the Roman commander took advantage of the Isthmian Games to proclaim "freedom" for all of these Greeks that the Romans had recently conquered—an announcement that was received by the assembled crowd with wide acclaim and wild rejoicing.[19] Throughout the Archaic, Classical, and Hellenistic periods, these Panhellenic sanctuaries and the Crown Games that were held there provided a way for the ancient Greek city-states to pursue diplomatic negotiations and for generals and commanders, like Alexander and Flamininus, to publicize popular decrees to large numbers of Greeks from throughout the Greek world. The Panhellenic nature of the sanctuaries was indeed a key component of their religious and social importance and offered opportunities for rare moments of unity in a society so often marked by division. In a society of such intense competition as the ancient Greeks created, it was both fitting and ironic that the sites of the Crown Games competitions should also serve as points of cultural unity.

During the great festivals of the Crown Games, the Panhellenic sanctuaries welcomed large numbers of pilgrims, spectators, vendors, athletes, trainers, and dignitaries, and those numbers increased over time as the games grew in popularity and prestige. Olympia featured a special building for hosting distinguished visitors, and the ordinary Greeks jostled with one another for open camping spaces and fresh water while navigating the sea of vendors selling food, souvenirs, firewood, sacrificial offerings, and anything else that might come in handy. In short, these sanctuaries were overrun for a few days every two or four years, and the archaeological record of these crowds sheds light on the experience of visiting one of the Crown Games festivals. Today, the sites of Delphi and Olympia routinely welcome impressive crowds of tourists, even if the material remains of these sites are poor compared to the splendor they once boasted. The reerection of some of the columns of the Temple of Zeus at Nemea offers a glimpse of the grandeur that the site once held, while the bare landscape at Isthmia betrays hardly a hint of the crowds and commotion that filled the sanctuary biennially over the course of hundreds of years in antiquity. With the conclusion of this introduction, it is time to examine the festivals themselves. What were the Crown Games, and what actually happened during a Crown Games festival? For some answers, I turn now to a closer examination of the Crown Games.

CHAPTER 1

Athletes, Festivals, and the Crown Games

I declare, I was victorious with my song and I carried away the eared tripod [as a prize].

—Hesiod, *Works and Days* 656–57

The Achaeans [Greeks] will carry his kleos far and wide, so that even those who have not yet been born will hear of it.

—Homer, *Odyssey* 3.203–4

Athletics and Ancient Greek Society

Ancient Greece featured a highly competitive culture steeped in contests of all kinds. From their earliest written records, the ancient Greeks described a society well versed in competition and victory. Their earliest poets, Homer and Hesiod, traditionally dated to the eighth century BCE, both display this competitive focus in their works. The two epic poems attributed to Homer, the *Iliad* and the *Odyssey*, feature athletic contests for their heroes to show off their strength and ability. In book 8 of the *Odyssey*, the hero Odysseus demonstrates his athletic prowess to his host Phaeacians by throwing a discus farther than any other man and then challenging any would-be rivals to compete against him in nearly any other contest.[1] Homer devotes the entirety of book 23 of the *Iliad* to describing the athletic contests sponsored by Achilles on the occasion of Patroclus's funeral. These two accounts are our earliest written records of ancient Greek athletic contests, and the events included running, boxing, wrestling, and a chariot race, among others. Homer's epics focus on the great deeds and adventures of the heroes involved in the Trojan War. However, Hesiod's *Works and Days* offers a more ordinary point of view of life in the early Archaic period, and like Homer's, his poetry reveals the importance of competition. In *Works and Days*, Hesiod boasts of his own victory in a poetry contest as part of the funeral games held for a ruler named Amphidamas at a site in northern Greece.[2] Clearly, even in the earliest days of the Archaic period, in the earliest surviving written sources, the Greeks were keen to compete.

Since at least the nineteenth century, modern scholars have characterized ancient Greece as an *agonistic* society—that is, the ancient Greeks created a culture that was intrinsically imbued with competition, whether politically, intellectually, or in events that we today would call athletics.[3] Although some scholars have rightly pointed out various drawbacks to and problems with this generalization of the ancient Greeks, the basic premise is on firm footing. Competition was an integral part of ancient Greek society, and athletic activity was a key component of ancient Greek culture in its broadest iterations. So thoroughly did athletic activity permeate Greek society that a community with aspirations to any kind of status had to possess an athletic facility for its citizens. Indeed, in his *Description of Greece*, Pausanias dismissed as irrelevant an obscure Greek settlement called Panopeus since it has no public buildings, no marketplace, no theater, and no gymnasium.[4] Athletics to the ancient Greeks were more than what we today might refer to as "games" or "amusements." The ancient Greek word meaning "to play" was not used in relation to athletic competition. Instead the Greeks used a word that referred to "struggles" (*agones*). For the ancient Greeks, athletics and competitions were not played. They were "struggled."[5]

Although athletic training and exercise were a staple of any Greek boy's education and upbringing, exceptionally talented athletes enjoyed opportunities to compete against elite athletes from their city, from their region, and from throughout the Greek world. A successful ancient Greek athlete could achieve a healthy income, a notable amount of acclaim, and a sizeable reputation through athletic victories. Local and regional festivals featured multiple athletic contests throughout the year. One scholar has recently identified evidence for 155 different athletic contests spanning the Archaic and Classical periods in ancient Greece.

It seems likely that more obscure contests and very local events offered even more opportunities for athletic competition.[6]

The Crown Games

Although each of the Crown Games possessed its own unique features, the games connected to the Olympian festival offered the basic program that the other sites for the most part subsequently adopted. Until the Romans came to Greece in the second century BCE, Panhellenic competitions were open to any free Greek male, but non-Greeks—pejoratively referred to as "barbarians"—were systematically excluded. One well-known story from the historian Herodotus relates how the Macedonian king Alexander I was barred from competing at Olympia in the early fifth century BCE as a non-Greek. Only when the king demonstrated his Greek origins as a descendant of the mythic (Greek) hero Heracles was he allowed to run in a race.[7] Crown Games competitions featured age categories for boys and adults, and the games at Isthmia and Nemea also offered a category for intermediate "beardless youths."[8] Girls and women were generally excluded from competing in person at the Crown Games, although they were eligible to send horses, jockeys, and chariot drivers to participate in the equestrian events. There is some uncertainty about girls' and women's ability to attend and observe the competitions, and I will revisit this issue in chapter 6.

Ancient Greek athletes who were victorious in the Crown Games commemorated their achievements in a variety of ways. Athletes who could afford the expense (or who had cities willing to help with the costs) could erect victory statues of themselves and commission epinician poems to proclaim their victories. While many festival games featured lucrative prizes and awards, at the Crown Games, the only official prize was a crown of branches and leaves: olive at Olympia, laurel at Delphi, pine at Isthmia (although for a while it was wild celery), and celery at Nemea. Although ancient literary accounts accuse foreign non-Greeks of scoffing at the triviality of such prizes, the writer Lucian notes that the crowns were merely "tokens" of an athlete's victory. The reputation that accompanied the crown was worth everything.[9] The crown was worn in ancient Greece on occasions of victory, praise, and thanksgiving in general, and ancient mythographers connected the crown to the story of the Titan Prometheus.

There are a few ancient Greek myths that incorporate the Titan Prometheus, but the best-known is probably the story where the trickster steals fire and gives it to humans, thus providing the technology that humanity needed to develop and thrive. As punishment for this theft, Zeus chains Prometheus to a rock and sends his eagle to repeatedly devour the Titan's regenerative liver. Eventually, though, Prometheus is freed with the help of Heracles. According to the early fifth-century-BCE Athenian tragedy writer Aeschylus, the crown symbolized the bonds of Prometheus and acted as a commemoration of the suffering he experienced to bring benefits to humankind.[10] The Roman-era mythographer Hyginus commented further, claiming that Prometheus established the crown as a commemoration for his victory and that "men established the custom of wearing crowns on occasions of supreme rejoicing and victories, and this can be seen in athletics and banquets."[11] Although it is unclear whether Aeschylus invented this origin of the crown or whether he was referring to a mythic precedent, it is clear that the Prometheus explanation for the crown was closely related to victory. In the myth, Prometheus wins his freedom from his bonds with the help of Heracles, but he also wears a crown as a symbolic bond, both to commemorate his victory and to demonstrate his acknowledgment of Zeus's authority. At Olympia, victorious athletes received olive crowns made from the trees that grew in the sacred precinct, and one tradition held that the olive tree in general, as well as the practice of awarding olive crowns at Olympia, had originated with the great hero Heracles.[12] Fittingly, Heracles also uses a crown of olive to ritually bind himself when he is freeing Prometheus.[13]

Classicist Leslie Kurke has argued that crowns were emblems of a victorious athlete's power, and the ritual "binding" of a victorious athlete placed the athletic performance in the category of sacrifice, similar to how animals were ritually bound before being killed. Victorious among humans but consecrated to a god, a "bound victor," or crowned athlete, held both a triumphant and a submissive position.[14] Honored and bound with fillets and ribbons, wearing a crown on his head, an athletic victor represented the best of mortals and suggested a special relationship with the divine.

Celebrating the Crown Games

In general, the preparation and observation of the festivals connected to the Crown Games featured a prescribed series of steps and procedures.

In 2003, the archaeologist and historian Stephen G. Miller published a very useful description of the logistics and processes that went into preparing and observing the Olympian festival as it was in the year 300 BCE.[15] Although the Olympian festival was just one of the four Crown Games, it is the best attested in the ancient sources. Despite the substantial changes applied over the centuries to the procedures for administering and holding the festival and games, Miller's reconstruction offers a practical beginning point for understanding the festival contexts of the Crown Games.

Several months before the games were scheduled to begin, judges were selected from among the citizens of the "host" or administrative city that cared for the nearby sanctuary. The city of Elis cared for the sanctuary at Olympia, although its right to do so was occasionally contested. Delphi managed the Pythian festival. Corinth was generally in charge of the Isthmian Games, and—for most of their history—the Nemean Games were administered by citizens of Argos. A few months before the games, heralds were sent to travel from city to city with notifications of the sacred truce, announcing the upcoming games and asserting the rights of athletes, trainers, spectators, and pilgrims to travel to the games in safety.[16] With the truce announcement, athletes began to journey to the administering cities. Once arrived, the competitors were required to train for an entire month under the watchful eyes of the judges, ensuring that only the most qualified athletes would make it to the Crown Games competitions.

While the athletes trained, the judges oversaw the various tasks and upgrades necessary to prepare the sites to host the games and their attendant crowds. Depending on the festival calendar, months or years might have elapsed since the running track was last tilled and smoothed, the hippodrome leveled, and other maintenance performed. A third-century-BCE inscription from Delphi lists the assignments meted out to various officials in preparation for the contests, which included digging and leveling athletic grounds, repairing a drain, shoring up retaining walls, and applying white plaster to various structures and buildings.[17] As in modern cities that host prestigious events and competitions, the organizers expended great care to ensure that the facilities looked just right.

On the appointed day at Olympia, the festival to Zeus kicked off with a large procession from Elis to the sanctuary of Olympia—about fifty-eight kilometers (ca. thirty-six miles).[18] The other Crown Games festivals presumably held similar processions, although their distances would have been shorter in length. For the Olympian festival, the judges, the athletes, the trainers, the horses and riders, the charioteers, the slaves, the family members, the pilgrims, the patrons, the civic officials, and any other enthusiasts present participated in a procession of people who likely numbered in the thousands. Presumably, the journey took a couple of days, with a night spent on the road. When the athletes arrived at the sanctuary of Zeus, they stood before a statue of Zeus alongside their fathers, brothers, and trainers, and they swore a sacred oath to commit no harm against the Olympian Games.[19] With the oath complete, the judges held a competition for trumpeters and heralds, and the winners earned the right to summon athletes and spectators to the contests and to publicly proclaim the names of the victors.[20]

Although the sanctuaries that hosted the Crown Games were crammed with buildings, dedications, colonnaded stoae, altars, and statues, the focal point of each sanctuary rested on the temple dedicated to its principal deity. At all four Crown Games sites, a large temple dominated the religious landscape and held a statue of the principal god. Although all four sanctuaries underwent renovations and revivals over the course of their histories, the basic outlines of the temples remained consistent. The style of these temples was "peripteral," a term that indicates that the temple itself was surrounded by columns on all four sides of its rectangular perimeter. Inside this colonnade was the naos, or temple itself, a closed building that housed the statue of the god. Individual temples varied from site to site, but in its basic form, the naos featured a pronaos, or antechamber, that was closed on three sides with its open side flanked by columns. From the pronaos, one could pass into the central chamber, an area closed off from the colonnade, called the cella (although sometimes the term "naos" is used to refer to this part of the temple more specifically). In the cella is where the statue of the god was placed, its size and majesty rendered more mysterious by the typical gloomy darkness of the room. Some cellae featured an additional room in the back, behind the statue, called an *adyton*, a word that means "forbidden," suggesting that the spot was more off limits than even the rest of the cella. The *adyton* of the Temple of Apollo at Delphi is where the priestess would sit to receive oracles from Apollo. Behind the cella and accessible only from the outside through the colonnade, some temples featured an opisthodomos, a sort of back porch.[21] Some temples featured lavish decorative friezes and bas-relief sculpture groups. The pediments were triangular-shaped areas above the columned exterior and often featured elaborate sculptural compositions. In addition, some temples featured sculptures on the metopes, the square-shaped panels above the columns of the interior naos building. At Olympia, the proportions of the Temple of Zeus called for six metopes above the entrance to the pronaos and six more on the other side of the temple, above the entrance to the opisthodomos.

Most ancient Greek temples oriented their entrances (and therefore the pronaos) toward the east. As the sun rose on a festival day, and the doors of the cella opened, the morning sun might illuminate the cult statue inside, if only for a moment. Only select priests and dignitaries could pass through the colonnade and the pronaos and enter the cella itself. Worship rituals took place in front of the temple at the altar or other designated sites, and most people were restricted to the colonnade, pronaos, and opisthodomos. The temple itself was the sanctuary of its god.

Returning to the Olympian festival: After the requisite number of sacrifices to the various deities who had shrines, altars, and temples in the sanctuary, the athletic competitions could begin under the watchful eye of robed officials. The *rhabdouchoi*, or "rod bearers," attended these judges and enforced rules by striking offenders with their rods.[22] The athletic competitions were a two- or three-day affair intermingled with more sacrifices—including perhaps a hecatomb offering of a hundred cattle to Zeus—celebratory banquets, sight-seeing, and spectacle.[23] Several modern treatments of the athletic program at Olympia offer comprehensive and systematic examinations of the competitions, rules, strategies, and techniques of ancient athletic events, and it will suffice here to mention only the fundamental components of a Crown Games athletic program.[24]

The main events associated today with athletic competition—contests of running, jumping, and throwing—were contested in the nude by the ancient Greeks. The Greek word for naked, *gymnos*, offers the root for the modern English word "gymnastics" as well as an understanding that the Greek gymnasium was the site for athletic training in the nude. Ancient sources offer competing explanations for the origins of nude athletic training and competition, none of which is very compelling. The ancient historian Thucydides claims that the Spartans were the first to remove their clothing and apply oil to their skin before exercising or competing in the nude and that, not so long before Thucydides's own day in the late fifth century BCE, athletes typically wore some kind of belt or strap across their waists.[25] Pausanias indicates that the eighth-century-BCE athlete Orsippus, from Megara, was the first to run naked and win at Olympia, and an inscription from long after the eighth century BCE recovered at Megara relates the same story.[26] The philosopher Plato credits (or blames) the people of Crete for introducing the Greeks to athletics and their attendant nudity.[27]

The running events in ancient Greek athletics were measured in stade lengths. The stadium at Olympia measured about 192 meters (about 210 yards), but the length of a stade varied from site to site.[28] The stade race was the original athletic event at Olympia, and over time, organizers added additional events. Besides the stade race, the Crown Games featured a two-stade-length race (called the diaulos), a long-distance race of about twenty-four stade lengths (the *dolichos*), and the *hoplitodromos*, a race in which the runners wore helmets and carried shields. Unlike in modern track stadiums, the runners did not circle in laps. A stade was much narrower than modern tracks. To keep the runners flowing smoothly, turning posts at one end (for the diaulos) or at both ends (for the *dolichos*) directed runners during their down-and-back races.

Besides the running events, there was the pentathlon, a competition of five events: a one-stade run, the long jump, the discus throw, the javelin throw, and wrestling. There were no competitions uniquely reserved for discus throwing, javelin throwing, and long jumping at the Crown Games. These events existed only as components of the pentathlon.

Combat sports, also contested in the nude, included boxing, wrestling, and pancratium. There were no divisions or classifications by weight. Robed referees controlled the events, and rules were enforced by flogging offenders with sticks. By the Hellenistic era (starting in the late fourth century BCE), boxers typically wrapped their hands with long leather straps, but these seem to have been intended to increase impact more than to protect the boxer's hands. There were no timed rounds, rings, or points. Boxers fought until one acknowledged defeat or became too dazed to continue. In wrestling, emphasis was placed on technique, grace, and style. Wrestling was contested upright, using only upper-body holds, with a fall occurring when one wrestler threw his opponent to the ground using a clean throw. The first to throw his opponent three times was declared the winner. The pancratium was the other combat sport in the ancient Olympian program. This was a potentially brutal event with few rules or inhibitions other than a prohibition against biting and eye gouging. The pancratium event ended when one of the athletes surrendered, lost consciousness, or (very rarely) died.

Musical competitions represented an important feature of the competitions at Delphi and other Crown Games sites. Although modern understandings of sport and athletics are dismissive of the nonphysical character of musical performances, winners in the ancient musical contests received victory crowns and enjoyed the honors of their victories. There is evidence for musical events and contests at Nemea and Isthmia, and the possibility of a theater at Olympia hints at a wider framework for these types of events in the Crown Games.

Finally, horse and chariot races were some of the most exciting and prestigious contests held at the Crown Games. There were several different equestrian events at Olympia by the fourth century BCE. These featured races for full-grown horses, colts, four-horse chariots, and two-horse chariots, in addition to the fifty-odd-year inclusion of a mule-cart race. The equestrian events took place in large flat hippodromes. Although no hippodrome from the ancient Greek world has been fully excavated, topography demanded that hippodromes varied in length from site to site. It is important to note that the victors of these events were the owners, not the riders or drivers, of the horses and chariots. A short poem by the third-century-BCE poet Posidippus offers a glimpse of the exciting nature of the equestrian races, the role of the referees, and the sacred nature of the festival's games. Posidippus's poem, written to commemorate a victory in the four-horse chariot race at the Pythian Games, describes a race where there was no clear winner. The judges decided that they would cast lots to determine the winner, trusting in Apollo to make known the chosen chariot. The lot fell to the chariot belonging to a man named Callicrates, of Samos, and the crowd roared its approval.[29]

Over the years, several events were added to or dropped from the athletic program at Olympia.[30] The first thirteen competitions at Olympia (traditionally dated from 776–728 BCE, but I will revisit this chronology) consisted of only one event: the stade race. In the games of the fourteenth Olympiad (724 BCE) the diaulos, a race of two stades, was added. Additional events were added (and occasionally dropped) over the ensuing centuries, including boys' events. Although the order of the athletic program at Olympia was fixed by the seventy-seventh Olympiad (472 BCE), events were still being added and subtracted during the Hellenistic age. For example, the games of the ninety-fifth Olympiad (400 BCE) featured horse racing with foal-drawn chariots for the first time. The sources are scantier for the athletic programs at the other Crown Games sites, but they presumably followed the Olympian lead, with the notable exception of the musical contests that figured so prominently in the Pythian Games.

These events, then, made up the athletic competitions at Olympia and, by extension, more or less at the rest of the Crown Games sites. Although the athletic spectacles were the most prominent and prestigious of the festival's events, there were plenty of other activities going on during a Crown Games festival. Indeed, the proximity of so many Greeks from all over the Mediterranean world offered enterprising Greeks a valuable marketplace for their ideas and a showcase for their talents.

At the Crown Games, philosophers, rhetoricians, orators, and poets offered performances and advertised their ideas and abilities to the masses assembled from throughout the Greek-speaking world. Stoae (covered walkways with attached rooms) and colonnades provided easy passage and welcome shade for sight-seeing tourists as they wandered around the sanctuaries admiring victory statues, reading votive dedications, and visiting treasuries, temples, and statues of the gods.

Banquet rooms and dining facilities at the Crown Games sites suggest lavish feasts and parties, given both to celebrate the victorious athletes and to draw attention to their hosts. In Plutarch's *Life of Themistocles*, we read that Themistocles the Athenian tried to outdo his political rival Cimon at Olympia by giving magnificent dinners and receiving his visitors in luxuriously furnished tents. As Plutarch tells it, Themistocles's plan backfired. Such overindulgence was expected of someone as rich and immature as Cimon, but the Greeks expected more of Themistocles and considered his extravagance gaudy and unseemly.[31] Luxurious tents and accommodations were the privilege of the wealthy, but enterprising merchants also showed off their finest at Olympia. According to the fourth-century-BCE writer Xenophon, during the Olympian Games, the sanctuary was filled with elaborate temporary booths and tents, presumably both to shield the visitors from the hot Peloponnesian summer sun and to entice them to make a purchase.[32]

The commotion of the crowds, the vendors, the performers, the announcements, and the bleating of animals on their way to the sacrificial altars, along with the heat of the August sun, must have been overwhelming at times at Olympia. It is no wonder that Pausanias tells us that the people of Elis regularly sacrificed to Zeus the Averter of Flies to drive out the flies from the sanctuary at Olympia. The Crown Games, then, were much more than merely a series of entertaining competitions. The festivals of the Crown Games offered a dizzying array of activity, spectacle, worship, and entertainment for visiting pilgrims and tourists. As the fourth-century-BCE speech writer Lysias declared, the Olympian contests—and we might extend this to the other Crown Games contests as well—were founded to be contests of bodies, rivalries of wealth, and displays of knowledge.[33]

The Religious Context of Greek Athletic Festivals

Before discussing the sites of the Crown Games, it will be useful to establish some foundational ideas for understanding the games and the competitions. The first of these ideas is the nature of ancient Greek religion and religious festivals. Any discussion of ancient Greek religion is bound to be complex, and a thorough treatment of the issue is beyond the scope of this book. Indeed, ancient Greek religion was feathered with intricate layers of nuance and idiosyncrasies as each city-state observed its own festival calendar, worshiped its own version of the Olympian deities and local heroes, and clung to its own mythologies, etiologies, and cultic rites. However, because of the Panhellenic nature of the four Crown Games sites, it is possible to generalize the typical observance of the religious festivals connected to the sanctuaries and the games.

Contemporary conceptions of religious observance typically focus on ideas such as conversion, faith, salvation, or the reassurance of divine assistance in troubling times. While these types of experiences could be found in ancient Greek mystery cults, philosophical schools, and in other endeavors, it is necessary to conceive of the public religious festival primarily as a civic event. An ancient Greek religious festival had more in common with the American observance of the Fourth of July (Independence Day) than a Christian mass or a Muslim congregational prayer. Throughout the ancient Greek world (not just at the Crown Games), festival observances typically included a procession, an animal sacrifice, and a communal meal as the elaborate rituals usually allowed the human participants to enjoy a substantial portion of the sacrificial meat. Indeed, as the noted scholar of ancient religion H. W. Parke has pointed out, for the ancient Greeks, eating the meat of the sacrificed animal was part of the ceremony—not a reverent act akin to a "sacramental communion" but more like "eating roast turkey at Christmas."[34] Much as Independence Day traditions such as town parades, midday barbecues, fireworks at night, and sundry civic celebrations might create a sense of unity in small-town America, an ancient Greek religious festival created a shared experience and a communal identity among those in attendance. Thus, it is inappropriate to speak of "conversion" or "belief" in this context. Participation in an ancient Greek religious festival was more of an expression of common ideals and civic identity than a profession of faith or an attempt to secure individual salvation.

Although the sense of religious devotion was quite different among the ancient Greeks than among typical religious worshippers today, it is important to remember that all ancient Greek athletic competitions, including and especially the Crown Games, were held in conjunction with a religious festival. The noted historian of ancient Greek religion Walter Burkert observes that in the ancient Greek language, the concept of religion and religious worship is characterized only by the vague term "honours of the gods."[35] Honoring the gods represented the overall aim of the festivals, and any athletic program contributed to this objective. Athletic competitions in the Crown Games were intended to honor the gods, and human endeavors in the Crown Games should be interpreted as offerings to deities. Only the finest specimens and best performances were worthy of victory in the sacred games.[36] While the human competitors and their hangers-on understandably looked to their own reputations and honors in the athletic competitions, the overarching context of the games was one of religious honors to a designated deity. In this way, the Olympian Games honored Zeus, as did the Nemean Games. At Delphi, the Pythian Games worshipped Apollo, and at Isthmia, the ancient Greeks honored Poseidon, the god of the sea.

The second key idea for understanding the Crown Games festivals is that, while each of the Crown Games honored a particular deity in conjunction with a religious festival, ancient Greek athletes sought to accumulate their own honors and augment their own reputations through athletic victory. The prestige of a Crown Games victory brought an immense amount of reputation to an ancient Greek athlete. Athletes vied with one another in pursuit of *arete*. *Arete* is a distinctly Greek term and concept without a precise English translation. Stephen G. Miller, defined *arete* as including "virtue, skill, prowess, pride, excellence, valor, and nobility," but Miller acknowledged that even all of those terms together did not completely fulfill the word's meaning.[37] Whether *arete* was gained through victory in athletics, battle, or other endeavors or whether it was an intrinsic character trait that could be revealed through such accomplishments was a question for the philosophers.[38] Either way, *arete* represented one of the fundamental elements of ancient Greek athletic competitions. Victory was inherently connected to an individual's *arete*, and the possession of *arete* brought esteem, honors, and reputation—a concept best encapsulated by the ancient Greek word *kleos*.

The term *kleos* refers to the fame, glory, and reputation that attended victory and represented the currency of victory. The heroes of ancient Greek myth sought *kleos* through victory, whether in battle, athletics, or the successful completion of challenging tasks or "labors." For mortal athletes, the *kleos* that accompanied an illustrious athletic victory, such as in the Crown Games, allowed the athlete to proclaim his (or, occasionally, her) victory even to those not present at the event. In a world before highlight reels, *SportsCenter*, social media, or newspaper sports sections, an athlete's *kleos* represented a claim to an undying reputation. The Greeks seem to have had a fairly grim conception of what the afterlife would bring. *Kleos* amassed and acquired in life, however, would continue to resonate long after an athlete's life had ended. In some cases (to be examined in chapter 6), extraordinary and powerful athletes secured some measure of immortal status and were worshipped after their deaths. Although a mortal athlete could personally do little to ensure the observation of cultic rites after death, a victorious athlete sought to amass *kleos* and receive the honors of a hero in his own lifetime.

But *kleos* required more than a triumphant victory won by an extraordinary athlete. It required an agent to publicize the famous deeds and a listening audience to adore and approve of the heroic feats. *Kleos* can only be possessed if someone proclaims it and someone else hears about it.[39] In all likelihood, the word *kleos* is etymologically related to the ancient Greek word that meant "to hear."[40] Commemoration before a wide audience was an important part of amassing *kleos*. *Kleos*, then, consisted of "wide fame" or "broad report" of tremendous deeds, commemorated and publicized aloud.[41] Since their *kleos* was so heavily dependent on the publication and dissemination of news of their great deeds, victorious athletes or their families often commissioned dedicatory statues and epinician poetry, such as the odes of Pindar and Bacchylides, to commemorate their victories and to publicize their *kleos*.

A third element in understanding the athletes, victors, and archaeology of the Crown Games is the role of myth, heroes, and immortality. All four of the Crown Games sites prominently featured a tomb of a (mythic) mortal hero. Although these figures had experienced death, they somehow continued to exert influence among the living. In this sense, they were immortal, although they most certainly had died.

Literary and archaeological sources reveal that the heroes supposedly buried at these sites were worshipped as part of the Crown Games festivals. It is difficult to define the ancient Greek *hero*. While modern connotations of the word "hero" evoke images of brave firefighters or comic book figures, the Greek heroes were a class of beings that occupied some kind of intermediate station between the mortal humans and the immortal gods, although specifying the boundaries is problematic.[42] Nevertheless, heroes accomplished great feats or achievements in life, frequently referred to in ancient sources as "labors," or, in Greek, *athla*, a term that etymologically connects the heroic deeds with athletic achievement.

The most obvious sign of heroic status was the institution of an honorific cult, most often at the hero's tomb, which indicated that, although the person had died, the figure had somehow passed from the mortal realm to the immortal. Despite considerable difficulties in understanding the various designations, nuances, criteria, and honors reserved for the ancient Greek cult of heroes, there is one general characteristic that all heroes possessed. The ancient Greeks believed that those with this intermediate, heroic status retained interest in and exerted influence on life on earth after death and therefore merited ritual and propitiation from mortals. At all four of the Crown Games sites, the veneration of a hero closely connected the athletes and the gods and suggested the possibility for mortals to earn some kind of immortal status through athletic achievement and its attendant *arete* and *kleos*.

An ancient commentator on Pindar's *Isthmian* odes noted that "all ancient games are for someone who has died."[43] While this seems an oversimplification, there existed strong connections between funerary honors, hero tombs, and Panhellenic competitions in ancient Greece. The architectural arrangements of the Panhellenic sanctuaries underscored the relationships between heroes, athletes, and immortality. At each of the four sites of the Panhellenic Crown Games, the hero's tomb and the shrine to the deity honored at the site were in close proximity to the competition grounds, linking the competitive athletic space with the sacred space of the sanctuary. This physical relationship between athletes, heroes, and the sacred space of a deity meant that those who competed did so in the shadow of a departed hero, a hero whose *kleos* lived on and who continued to receive cultic honors. The stories of the heroes extended the limits of human experience, providing a vehicle for the best humans to achieve some measure of divinity, though falling short, of course, of equality with the gods of Mount Olympus. The hero was an extraordinary figure who transcended the normal boundaries between mortality and immortality, humanity and divinity. These figures, commemorated in myth and memorial, provided the paradigms for humans seeking some measure of immortality through athletics.

These three foundational ideas—the games' religious context, athletes' quest for *arete* and *kleos*, and the role of the hero in the Crown Games—offer the conceptual framework for understanding the Crown Games competitions in their greater context. The games honored the gods, and athletic performances were part of the sacrifices and offerings that accompanied the festival setting. Victorious athletes demonstrated *arete* and proclaimed their *kleos* in visual and poetic art, ensuring that their reputations would outstrip their travels and outlast their life spans. All four of the Crown Games sites prominently featured hero tombs and hero cults in close proximity to the athletic facilities, and the presence of the hero's tomb offered a paradigm of how athletes could strive for some measure of immortality via heroic cult. Furthermore, an extraordinary few actually managed to secure heroic cult through their *kleos* and *arete*. With these principles in mind, we are ready to engage with the festivals and their locations. We turn first to Olympia, the site of the most prestigious of the Crown Games.

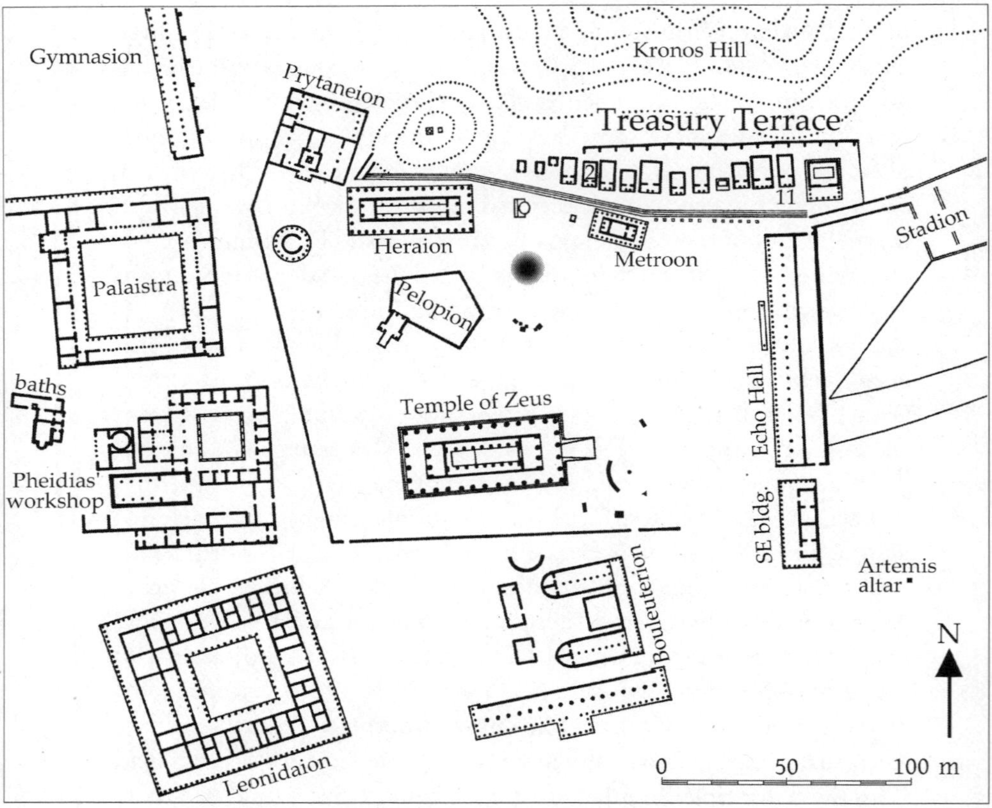

Site plan of ancient Olympia. Courtesy Hans R. Goette.

CHAPTER 2

Olympia and the Olympian Games

We know that the growth of Olympia's fame came from the festival crowds and the Olympian contests.

—Strabo, *Geography* 8.3.30

O Olympia, mother of gold-crowning contests.

—Pindar, *Olympian* 8.1

At Olympia, a site situated at the confluence of the Cladeus and Alpheus Rivers in the northwest Peloponnese, the ancient Greeks held quadrennial athletic games to honor the god Zeus. Although the Olympian Games took place over a handful of days every four years, nevertheless, the site of Olympia was utilized year-round as a Panhellenic sanctuary for worship and commemoration. According to the Roman-era writer Pausanias, the earliest stories about Olympia held that "people of the golden age," who predated today's human race, made a shrine there to Kronos, the father of Zeus.[1] Archaeology suggests less spectacular origins: human settlements at Olympia stretch back into the Bronze Age, to the middle of the third millennium BCE.

Votive bronzes indicate that, long before the site of Olympia hosted organized athletic competitions, there existed there some kind of shrine to Zeus, and ancient literary sources mention the presence of an oracle used to consult the will of the gods.[2] During Greece's Archaic age (ca. 800–480 BCE), the site was transformed into a Panhellenic religious sanctuary that was organized around the worship of Zeus. Although there were disputes over which nearby city should hold the right to manage the sanctuary and the games, for most of the sanctuary's history, the temples, shrines, and games were administered by the people of Elis, the nearest prominent city-state. It was at Elis that, every four years during the month of August, athletes and spectators from throughout the ancient Greek world assembled for the Olympian Games. Traditionally, the date of the foundation of the ancient Olympian Games has been fixed at 776 BCE, but archaeology continually argues for a later date, perhaps as late as 700 BCE.[3] By the Classical period of Greek history (480–323 BCE), the Olympian Games boasted an elaborate athletic program and offered the most prestigious venue for ambitious competitors. Athletes who won at Olympia could enjoy the *kleos*, or glory, of victory at the highest level. Victorious athletes associated themselves with the gods and heroes of Olympia in their quests for undying glory, and the material record underscores the strong connections at Olympia between gods, heroes, and athletic victory.

Olympia: The Altis

Modern visitors are indebted to the detailed, if occasionally roundabout, description of ancient Olympia written by the Roman-era traveler Pausanias in the second century CE. In his *Description of Greece*, Pausanias dedicated two of its ten books to exploring Olympia and the surrounding area. As he wrote, "There are many wondrous and worthwhile things to see and hear about in Greece," but the games at Olympia enjoyed a special amount "of divine attention."[4] His description of the buildings, monuments, statues, and other components of the sacred site is especially valuable since many of these features have been lost through time. Besides the literary record, we know about ancient Olympia from the archaeological record. German archaeologists began excavating the Panhellenic site of Olympia in the late nineteenth century. The 1936 Olympic Games in Berlin jump-started efforts to renew the excavations, and from 1937 to 1966, a considerable portion of the sanctuary, including the stadium, was excavated completely.[5] By the 1950s, the excavators were able to reconstruct various phases of the stadium's construction.[6] Ongoing excavations, publications, and research at Olympia continue to expand our understanding of the sanctuary.

With over 140 years of systematic and scholarly examination of the site, the corpus of modern scholarship treating Olympia is appropriately deep and rich. Archaeologists, classicists, historians, art historians, kinesiologists—and surely scholars in many other fields as well—have contributed to modern interpretations and understandings of this ancient site and its uses, deploying a variety of disciplinary techniques and theoretical frameworks while grappling with Olympia's archaeological, epigraphic, numismatic, historical, and artistic sources. Rather than synthesize and address all of the features and scholarly components of this enormous site, for now we will focus on the main buildings, the important monuments, and a generalized treatment of the site's religious and athletic features. Somewhat confusingly for the modern visitor, the nature of archaeological excavations situates building foundations and features side by side even if those architectural features might have been built hundreds of years apart. The sanctuary at Olympia grew and developed throughout its history, and many buildings were remodeled or altered significantly over the years. The site boasted its greatest number of buildings during the Roman era.

Over time, the sanctuary at Olympia acquired many buildings for the rituals connected to the cult of Zeus, the worship of other deities, and the athletic festivals. By the Hellenistic period, there were a gymnasium and a palaestra on the west side of the sanctuary, intended to be used by athletes for practice and warm-up during the festival. Farther south lay a large guesthouse, called the Leonidaion, which hosted visiting dignitaries. Unique to Olympia, this building was the gift of a private citizen, a man named Leonidas, the son of Leotas of Naxos.[7]

Another of the buildings at the west end of the sanctuary at Olympia, called today Pheidias's Workshop, held the artist's tools used for creating the immense cult statue of Zeus that sat in the Temple of Zeus. In addition, Olympia featured a group of so-called treasuries. As E. Norman Gardiner points out, the name "treasury" is a bit misleading since these buildings were not built merely with the purpose of holding treasures. Rather, these buildings acted as dedications from individual city-states. In a society as competitive as ancient Greece, treasuries offered another opportunity for cities to demonstrate their prosperity and bolster their reputations by showcasing elaborate workmanship and splendid wealth. Gardiner characterizes the treasuries as "a lasting witness to the Panhellenic character" of the site at Olympia.[8] A city's treasury advertised its city's prominence, side by side with the treasuries of other cities.

Besides the treasuries, victory and votive dedications, and colonnades at Olympia, the site also featured a council house (Bouleuterion) and other buildings used to administer the Olympian festival. Excavations identified the Bouleuterion at Olympia in the late nineteenth century. The remains suggest a strangely shaped building featuring a double apse and a central area that might have held a large statue.[9] According to Pausanias, the Bouleuterion featured a statue of Zeus holding a thunderbolt before which Olympian athletes, their male relatives, and their trainers swore oaths to do no harm to the Olympian Games and that they had been in strict training for the previous ten months.[10] The Olympian Boule—the council that met in the Bouleuterion—was in charge of administering the games, rendering judgments, and voting honors to benefactors.

Although its workings are obscure, Pausanias offers a clue about the boule's activities. According to Pausanias's account, in the fourth century BCE, the Athenian historian Xenophon was awarded land near Olympia that was contested between the Spartans and the Eleans. The Olympian Boule acted as judge in this dispute. Although Pausanias does not mention the actual deliberations or decision of the boule, he reports that the Eleans pardoned Xenophon and he was allowed to live on the contested land.[11] Xenophon's experience suggests that the Olympian Boule played a role in mediating disputes between city-states, although this role was perhaps limited to issues in close proximity to the sanctuary. Multiple recovered inscriptions attest to the activity of the boule, and an early inscription suggests that, at times, the boule consisted of as many as five hundred members, although this seems like an unwieldly number for conducting the everyday business of the Olympian festival.[12] To what extent the *hellanodikai*, or "judges of the Greeks," who were recognized as the umpires for the games, collaborated with the Olympian Boule is unclear.[13]

The area containing the religious structures at Olympia was called the Altis, an ancient Greek name used exclusively at Olympia to designate the sacred area within the sanctuary. By the time of Pausanias in the second century CE, the Altis was crammed with statues of victorious athletes, dedicatory offerings, altars and shrines, treasuries, and various constructions of the Roman era.[14] An early sixth-century-BCE Doric temple probably was originally used to honor and worship Zeus and his sister-wife, Hera, jointly, but with the completion of the massive Temple of Zeus in the mid-fifth century BCE, this older structure was likely reassigned to Hera alone.[15] During the Olympian festival, the olive-wreath crowns were kept on a chryselephantine (i.e., fabricated from gold and ivory) table inside this temple of Hera, to be presented to the victors in the contests.[16]

The interior of the Temple of Zeus featured the massive chryselephantine statue of Zeus sculpted by the Athenian Pheidias, and this statue was one of the so-called wonders of the ancient world. The seated statue of Zeus featured gold and gems on its throne, as well as a golden cloak and sandals. Mythological motifs, including scenes with Heracles, Atlas, Theseus, Ajax, Prometheus, and others decorated the screens that shielded the statue from the rest of the temple. The seated Zeus wore a crown of olive branches and held a statue of the personified goddess Victory (Nike) in his right hand, a reminder to mortals that victory at Olympia was god-given. A fragmentary poem from the Hellenistic period gushes that the monetary value of the statue's splendor defied calculation.[17] Indeed, the ancient geographer Strabo notes that Pheidias might have miscalculated the statue's proportions: the seated Zeus was so large that, if Zeus were to stand, he would crash through the temple's roof. Strabo goes on to relate that, when asked what inspired his image of Zeus, the artist, Pheidias, quoted a line from Homer in which Zeus's nodding assent caused "great Olympus to quake."[18] Within the temple and its porch, dedications from kings and rulers, including Roman emperors, occupied privileged locations at the time of Pausanias's visit. In front of Zeus's temple, an immense altar, the altar of Olympian Zeus, made from ash mixed with water, ascended several meters into the air, and the residue from the daily sacrifices regularly added more material to the ashy construction.[19]

Between the Temple of Zeus and the Temple of Hera, a five-sided, mostly open-air shrine to the hero Pelops reminded ancient visitors to Olympia of the mythic origins of the Olympian Games.

Olympia: The Foundation Myth

The myth of Pelops enjoys a prominent place in the traditional origins of the Olympian Games.[20] According to this myth, young Pelops was killed by his father Tantalus, who disingenuously cooked and served the boy's body as a feast to the gods. When the gods discovered this crime, they resurrected the boy with minimal damage: the goddess Demeter had inadvertently partaken of the flesh, and Pelops had to make do with an ivory shoulder.[21] As one beloved of the gods (Pindar *Olympian* 1.71–81 relates that Pelops was the favorite of Poseidon) and as one who had overcome death, Pelops was an attractive figure for athletes who were seeking immortal honors. These divine favors corresponded with his athletic victory in a chariot race near Olympia.

According to the story, the local ruler named Oenomaus promised his daughter, Hippodameia, to anyone who could beat him in a chariot race, but the penalty for losing was swift execution. Twelve or so suitors, the exact number varies depending on the retelling, tried and failed, and Oenomaus fixed their severed heads above the door to his home.[22] Although the details of the race vary from version to version of the story, all agree that Pelops challenged and defeated King Oenomaus. During the contest, Oenomaus perished and Pelops claimed the girl and the kingdom.

The race of Pelops and Oenomaus served as one of the etiological foundation stories for the Olympian Games, and pieces of the Pelops myth were scattered throughout Olympia and its environs. For instance, the treasury of the city of Sicyon featured Pelops's gold-handled dagger, and the people of Elis claimed to have once possessed the hero's ivory shoulder blade—a talisman that was believed to have played a role in the Greeks winning the Trojan War. This shoulder blade, however, had disappeared by Pausanias's time.[23] The eastern pediment of the Temple of Zeus at Olympia, which was constructed during the fifth century BCE, featured this story's main characters as they readied their horses. In the sculpture group, Zeus stands between Pelops and Oenomaus, while Hippodameia and her mother Sterope stand to either side.[24] As the eastern pediment above the temple's "front door," the imagery would have been hard to ignore. According to Pausanias, after his victory, Pelops held the Olympian Games on an unprecedented and memorable scale, and later the great hero Heracles (known in Latin as Hercules) revived the games and instituted the practice of sacrificing to Pelops.[25] Heracles, in this account, designated the site of the five-sided shrine called the Pelopion, a sanctuary for remembering Pelops with cult and sacrifice.[26]

Nestled between the temples of Hera and Zeus, the Pelopion enjoyed a prominent position in the Altis. Although Pausanias made passing mention of a bronze chest near the (otherwise unknown) sanctuary of Artemis Kordax that housed the bones of Pelops, the Pelopion at Olympia is the site most often associated with the tomb of the hero.[27] Here, Pausanias reported, the Eleans honored Pelops with more than the customary rituals for departed heroes, and each year officials sacrificed a black ram to the hero.[28] In addition to his significance as an etiological hero for the games, Pelops and the Pelopion occupied an important location in close proximity to the actual site of the athletic contests. In *Olympian* 10, the ancient Greek poet Pindar recounts how the laws of Zeus compelled him to sing about the "contests" that Heracles established "near the ancient tomb-marker of Pelops."[29] As at the other Panhellenic sanctuaries, the site of the athletic competitions was prominently placed near the tomb of a dead (mythic) hero, juxtaposing the contests of the athletes with the memory of the hero.

German archaeologists excavated and reexcavated the Pelopion several times between the 1920s and the 1990s. These excavations confirmed that beneath the Classical-period Pelopion, there is a large round, mound-shaped structure that dates back to the Bronze Age.[30] However, it is much too early to be connected to the traditional mythology of the Mycenaean-era Pelops. This Bronze Age tumulus, measuring twenty-seven meters in diameter, was constructed sometime around 2600–2500 BCE and is therefore at least a thousand years too old to be a late Bronze Age Mycenaean construction, and was erected around 1700 years before the traditional date of the foundation of the games at Olympia. Later inhabitants of Olympia, during the middle Bronze Age, built a series of houses around and on top of portions of the site of the tumulus, suggesting that the significance of the tumulus had diminished. Although there was a tumulus monument on the site of the Pelopion during much of the Bronze Age and later, there is no archaeological indication of a religious cult or ritual on this spot during the late Bronze Age, or Mycenaean period, when the mythic Pelops was supposed to have lived. It seems that only later did the myth of Pelops arrive at Olympia.[31]

Excavations revealed that there was a clear break between the Bronze Age tumulus and houses and the erection of the Classical-period five-sided Pelopion structure. A wide layer of evenly distributed ash, soil, and charcoal, dated to around 600 BCE, suggests a general reorganization of the entire sanctuary, and the cult of Pelops may have been introduced at this time.[32] In 600 BCE, there might have been some surviving, timeworn remnants of the nearly two-thousand-year-old Bronze Age tumulus to draw the attention of those who visited Olympia as a reminder of the heroic age, but there is no evidence of a cult of Pelops before this layer of ash was laid down. Most likely, the story of Pelops was imposed on the visible remains of the ancient Bronze Age tumulus, perhaps around this time of reorganization around 600 BCE. In other

The stadium at Olympia. Author's photograph.

words, it seems that the Pelops myth at Olympia was connected to this mound, which was identified as his tomb around two thousand years after the mound had been erected.

Certainly, the ancient Greeks of the Classical period accepted the Pelopion as the tomb of Pelops. Whether or not the body of a person known as Pelops was actually under the ground of the sanctuary (no evidence of a burial was found in the tumulus) is less important than the knowledge that the ancient Greeks, at least from the time of the poet Pindar in the early Classical period and perhaps as early as the site reorganization of circa 600 BCE, accepted the tomb as the authentic resting place of the mythic hero Pelops. The evidence discussed here suggests that the Greeks appropriated the visible remains of the ancient tumulus for Pelops at a time when the sanctuary and contests were expanding in importance.[33]

The placement of a hero's tomb next to the site of the competitions is a common feature at athletic sites throughout ancient Greece, including at the Crown Games sites, and it is possible that this feature originated at Olympia. Archaeological excavations have revealed that Olympia's original stadium was situated very close to the hero tomb of Pelops.

Olympia: The Stadium

The present site of Olympia's stadium is just to the east of the Altis, artfully separated from the sanctuary by the remains of the Echo Colonnade and the arched stadium entrance. This version of the stadium, dubbed by archaeologists "Classical Stadium III," has been dated to the end of the Classical period, to around 340 BCE.[34] Excavations have shown that the earlier two stadiums, as well as a possible even earlier "Ur-Stadium," were situated just about ninety meters to the west, placing the western edge of the racetrack firmly within the Altis.[35] Although the experts disagree on the exact details, it is clear enough that the earliest stadiums at Olympia were closely attached to the Altis. Relying on excavated wells (which were used for drinking water) and a portion of a retaining wall that has been dated to the time of Stadium I, Eric Brulotte determined that this early stadium ended only about fifty meters from the southeast edge of the Pelopion. In 1994, Brulotte suggested that the turning post for this stadium was remembered as the pillar from the house of Oenomaus mentioned in Pausanias 5.20.7.[36]

Archaeology confirms that the earliest running track at Olympia was physically connected to the Altis. Philostratus, a late but not necessarily unreliable source, from the second and third centuries CE, claims that the stade race—the original event of the Olympian contests—originated with runners standing a stadium's length from the altar of Zeus. As the runners took off racing, he says, they ran toward the priest of Zeus, with the winner receiving the honor of lighting the sacrificial offerings.[37] This account indicates that the original Olympian contest—the one-stade race—began at the stadium's eastern end, with the runners sprinting toward a finish line in the Altis and close to the Pelopion. The tomb of the hero on the edge of the racetrack would have connected the hero's presence with the competitions.

Although the large altar of Zeus would have figured prominently in the view of those spectators in this early stadium who were watching the finish line in the Altis, the tumulus mound that eventually marked the resting place of Pelops would have been ever present for both athletes and spectators.[38] The proximity of the hero Pelops allowed ancient Greek athletes to compare their feats with his, and reminded both the competitors and the spectators that great victories in athletic contests could extend an athlete's power beyond the end of life. Thus, a tomb near an athletic site, especially a site as prestigious as Olympia, brought honor to the interred and inspiration to the competitors.

Hippodameia and the Heraia at Olympia

Pausanias informs his readers that, in addition to the tomb of Pelops, the tomb of Pelops's wife, Hippodameia, was also located in the Altis at Olympia and that it enjoyed a similar, albeit more limited, relationship with athletics. According to Pausanias, the Hippodameion was surrounded by a wall and situated near the processional entry to the Altis. Here, supposedly, the bones of Hippodameia were interred by ancient Greeks after an oracle commanded them to be brought back from the region of Argos in the northeast Peloponnese.[39] Although archaeology has yet to reveal any material remains of Hippodameia's tomb or shrine at Olympia, Pausanias connected this mythic woman to the celebration of the festival of Hera, the Heraia, which was celebrated every four years at Olympia.

Pausanias writes that, every fourth year, sixteen women from the area around Olympia wove a robe for the statue of Hera and held games called the Heraia.[40] Similar to the games of the first several Olympian festivals, the athletic component of the Heraia consisted of a footrace in the stadium for three different age groups of unmarried girls. Presumably, these groups of girls would have been children and teenagers. The distance for these races was shortened by about one-sixth, a measurement in proportion to the difference between the size of the Temple of Hera and the larger Temple of Zeus within the Altis.[41] The three victorious girls received olive crowns and a portion of the sacrificial beef, and they earned the right to dedicate images of themselves at Olympia with their names inscribed on them. Rather than compete in the nude like the male athletes at Olympia, girls in the Heraia wore a short garment that ended above the knees and exposed one breast.

As Pausanias, our only substantial source for the Heraia, relates it, it was Hippodameia who instituted the festival, including its footraces for girls, in thanks for Pelops's victory in the chariot race that had assured their marriage. In addition to the footraces for Hera, those celebrating the Heraia at Olympia honored Hippodameia and the memory of another local woman named Physkoa each with a dance.[42] The lack of surviving physical remains for any kind of shrine or tomb makes it difficult to assign a date to the cult of Hippodameia at Olympia or to the institution of the *Heraia*. Unhelpfully, Pausanias offers only that the heroine's bones were brought to Olympia "later" (i.e., after Hippodameia left Olympia) and that the games for the girls were instituted "long ago."[43]

Until more information about the cult of Hippodameia at Olympia surfaces, many questions, including the time of its institution, will remain. Nevertheless, from what we do know, the relationship between Hippodameia, her tomb, and the festival and races of the Heraia correspond loosely to the relationship between the myth and shrine of Pelops and the Olympian Games. Despite the thematic similarities the Heraia might have shared with the contests for males at the Olympian Games, parallel festivals elsewhere in ancient Greece that were reserved for unmarried girls imply that the Heraia was fundamentally different from the contests of the Crown Games. The running contests of the Heraia served an initiatory function for the girls and young women, quite different from the purpose of the male-only Olympian contests. The role of the Heraia as an initiation festival for soon-to-be-married girls hints at a very ancient origin, although the athletic component might have been introduced around the time of Olympia's reorganization. One scholar has suggested that the institution of a committee of sixteen women to oversee Hera's festival took place at the same time as the development of the Panhellenic Crown Games circuit around 580 BCE.[44] While the footraces of the Heraia are probably more accurately classified as initiation rites for unmarried girls than as full-fledged athletic competitions, the connection between heroic tomb and athletic competition was deliberate and underscores the important connections between heroic cult and festival games.

At Olympia, the presence of Pelops and Hippodameia on the pediment sculptures of Zeus's temple, as well as their tombs in the Altis, oriented toward the stadium, connected the athletics of the living with the veneration and feats of the dead. Elite ancient Greek athletes, competing in close proximity to these memorials, were constantly reminded of heroic accomplishments from mythic times and perhaps sought to measure their own accomplishments against those of the heroes.

Besides the tombs of the heroes on the Altis, there were other tombs near the athletic grounds at Olympia. Pausanias notes that Endymion, one of the heroic progenitors of the Elean people, was interred near the end of the stadium at Olympia. According to the story, Endymion was a grandson of Zeus and had his three sons compete in a race, promising his kingdom to the winner.[45] In addition to this tradition, Pausanias describes a mound of earth in the hippodrome, south of the stadium, called the "Taraxippus" or the "terror of horses."[46] The location of this mound coincided with a spot on the racetrack where horses were prone to panic for no apparent reason, but it is unclear exactly what the Taraxippus was. Pausanias provides several possible explanations, and most of them assume the mound to be some kind of tomb that was haunted by a restless spirit. As we saw with the Pelopion and the earliest stadium, this mound in the hippodrome indicated a place where the world of the dead intersected with the competitions of the living, and this belief in restless spirits leaving their nearby tombs to cause hippodrome accidents might have been widespread in ancient Greece.[47] Again, the presence of a tomb near the competition site emphasized the power that the departed heroes continued to exert on the world of the living.

Heracles, Athla, *and Olympia*

Of all the ancient heroes, the Greeks perhaps considered Heracles the most important, the most famous. At Olympia, the Greeks recognized and worshiped Heracles simultaneously as a (re)founder of the games, a victorious athlete, and a model for human athletes. Heracles is a complex figure in ancient Greek myth. Versions of his origins and exploits abounded in the ancient Greek world. Early Greek poetry (Homer, Hesiod, and the *Homeric Hymn to Heracles*) situates his birth at Thebes and describes it as the result of a union between the mortal Alcmene and immortal Zeus, but later accounts (e.g., Herodotus) place the infant Heracles in Phoenicia and Crete.[48] As Pausanias writes (much later), the version of Heracles who came to Greece from Crete held games at Olympia and introduced the wild olive crown as a prize. Tradition held that in these mythic games arranged by Heracles, the gods themselves had competed, with Zeus himself wrestling there and Apollo winning a footrace against Hermes.[49]

As a mighty hero who had achieved immortal status through his great deeds, Heracles was a figure who emphasized athletic achievement for the ancient Greeks. The exploits of Heracles were filled with athletic activities. According to the ancient mythographer Apollodorus, Heracles enjoyed an upbringing suitable for Greek aristocratic mortals. As a youth, he learned to drive a chariot, wrestle, use weapons, and play the lyre—all components of ancient athletic competitions. Heracles was most often considered a wrestler, and several mythic episodes recounted his prowess in this sport. Apollodorus reports that Heracles killed Polygonus and Telegonus, both grandsons of Poseidon, in a wrestling match. When the Sicilian hero Eryx challenged Heracles to a wrestling bout for one of Geryon's cattle that had escaped and joined Eryx's herd, Heracles killed him on his third throw. When Heracles came across Antaeus, a son of Poseidon who killed strangers by wrestling them to death, the great hero killed Antaeus in a wrestling match by preventing him from touching the ground, from which he drew his strength. Heracles even wrestled in the underworld, breaking the ribs of Menoetes, who tended Hades's cattle and had objected to Heracles's slaughter of a cow to provide blood for the shades of the dead.[50]

In all these instances, mainly reported by Apollodorus, Heracles engaged in athletic contests with opponents he happened to meet during his journeys. Those who challenged Heracles to wrestle received the worst of it, in most cases death. This characterization of Heracles as a journeying wrestler held great cultural significance for the ancient Greeks. He demonstrated his prowess and *arete* through athletic competition, chiefly wrestling, and ancient Greek athletes sought to do the same. In addition to highlighting these competitive athletic endeavors, Heracles and his adventures represented a broader conception of athleticism that was common for the ancient Greek hero, a concept based on struggle, adversity, triumph, and prizes.

Ancient literary sources often used athletic terminology to describe Heracles's exploits.[51] Isocrates, the fourth-century-BCE Athenian rhetorician, described Heracles's life as full of "contests" (*agones*).[52] The best known of Heracles's adventures, the so-called "twelve labors," are most commonly associated with his service to Eurystheus in penance for the blood guilt the hero incurred from the murder of his own children. Many ancient writers called Heracles's labors *athla*, an ancient Greek word that denoted competitive struggle but literally referred to prizes or contests for prizes (and the root of modern words like "athlete" and "athletics"). The *athla* of Heracles characterize him as a figurative "athlete" who struggled for his "prizes." These labors were literally *athletic* contests. Heracles's labors were indicative of the ancient Greek understanding of competition: remember, the ancient Greeks did not "play" their games; they struggled them. Like athletic competitions, Heracles's labors, or *athla*, are best understood as "struggles" or competitions for a prize.

At Olympia, the feats of Heracles were captured and commemorated in close conjunction with the most important building in the Altis—the Temple of Zeus. The metopes of the great temple featured relief sculptures of twelve of Heracles's labors, and it is likely that these metopes played a key role in the conceptualization of Heracles as an athlete in the ancient Greek world. Classicist Wendy J. Raschke has noted the similarities between the poses and depictions of the figure of Heracles in these relief sculptures and other images of athletic victors and victories from the ancient Greek world. Ancient Greek poets explicitly connected Heracles's immortality with the completion of his labors. Of all of the prizes won through his athletic (in both senses of this word) victories, the most valuable was immortality. Well-accomplished labors (*athla*) brought this ultimate prize. As Rashke concludes, the immortality earned by Heracles acted as "an appropriate lesson" for the mortal athletes who competed in their own "labors" at Olympia.[53]

Consistent with the exploits of Heracles and the power of athletic victory, athletes and dynasts sought to stake their own claims to heroic honors in the Altis at Olympia. Well aware of the glory and renown that came with victory at Olympia, King Philip II of Macedon, the father of Alexander the Great and the architect of Macedon's fourth-century-BCE ascendance in the Greek world, paid close attention to the Olympian Games. Philip's horses won an Olympian victory in 356 BCE, a triumph that Philip proudly featured on Macedonian coinage.[54] Philip's victory at Olympia was a notable feat in its own right, but it was the construction of a dynastic shrine or temple in the Altis at Olympia that was intended to perpetuate Philip's reputation among the Greeks.

The Philippeion

Sometime after conquering much of Greece at the Battle of Chaeronea in 338 BCE, Philip commissioned the Philippeion at Olympia. Pausanias describes the Philippeion as a round building made of brick, surrounded by columns, and archaeologists have located this building in the Altis directly west of the temple of Hera. Within this structure were placed statues that appeared to be made of gold and ivory, depicting Philip and his family: his father, Amyntas; his mother, Eurydice; his wife, Olympias; and his son Alexander the Great. Although the statues inside the Philippeion are better described as dynastic portraits than as religious cult statues, the monument's placement inside the Altis staked out important ground within the sanctuary, terrain usually reserved for the commemoration of gods, heroes, and athletic victors. Indeed, one modern scholar has noted that the chryselephantine appearance of the statues located in "the most revered temenos [sanctuary] of the Greek mainland" made an "extraordinary—even revolutionary—for their time" statement about Philip and his family.[55]

Situating this monument within the Altis was a clear statement connecting King Philip and his family to the prestige of the gods, heroes, and athletic victors at Olympia. As Elizabeth D. Carney, a historian of the Hellenistic period, notes, the chryselephantine images, a medium typically reserved for statues of the gods, "hinted at the divinity of Philip's family, but did not proclaim it."[56] This building has been rightly interpreted as a monument to Philip's great victory at the Battle of Chaeronea. As a commemoration of victory, the Philippeion is consistent with the other offerings in the Altis but much more brazen in its message. The message of this building was the power of the Macedonian dynasty. As the leader of the Greeks, Philip had the building constructed to associate himself with divinity, kingship, and victory at Olympia. In addition to the magnificence of the Philippeion, the Eleans saw fit to honor Philip and Alexander, as well as the later Macedonian generals Seleucus and Antigonus, with statues at Olympia.[57]

Olympia as a Model

As Olympia developed into a Panhellenic sanctuary and the quadrennial games took on an increasingly prominent profile during Greece's Archaic period, other sanctuaries in Greece imitated both Olympia's design and athletic program. The sites of Nemea, Isthmia, and Delphi were reorganized during the early sixth century BCE, resulting in an increased emphasis on athletic competition. In addition, these other three sites juxtaposed hero cult and tomb with the sites of the athletic venues. As did Olympia, these Crown Games sites underscored the connections between athletic achievement and heroic honors. Following the cycle of the Crown Games, we turn to the Panhellenic sanctuary of Zeus at Nemea next.

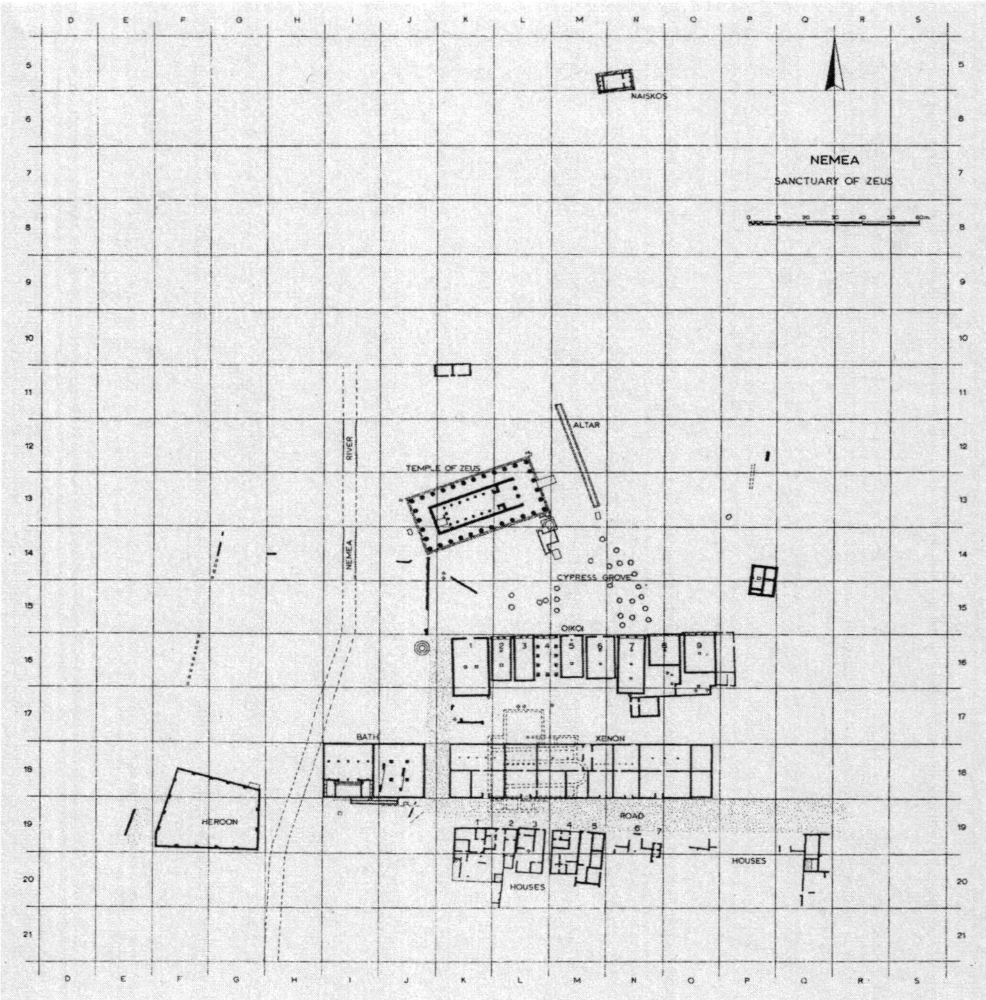

Site plan of ancient Nemea. From Stephen G. Miller, "Excavations at Nemea, 1984–1986," *Hesperia* 57 (1988): 2, fig. 1. Image courtesy of the Trustees of the American School of Classical Studies at Athens.

CHAPTER 3

Nemea and the Nemean Games

For the telling of a deed lives longer than its doing.
. . . May I set forth such a telling in honor of Zeus,
the son of Kronos, and in honor of Nemea.

—PINDAR, *NEMEAN* 4.6–9

The site of ancient Nemea, situated in the northeastern Peloponnese, roughly equidistant between Corinth and Argos, featured a sanctuary of Zeus and a Panhellenic athletic festival. Like the games at Isthmia and Delphi, the games at Nemea grew to Panhellenic status during the early sixth century BCE.

The Foundation Myth

In the most common version of the myth that treats the foundation of the Nemean Games, the seven heroes who marched against Thebes instituted the competitions as funeral games for a child named Opheltes.[1] On their way to Thebes, the seven stopped in Nemea, where a king named Lycurgus reigned with his wife, Eurydice. According to an oracle's command, their infant son Opheltes was not to be allowed to touch the ground until he was (paradoxically) able to walk.

Unaware of the oracle, the seven met Hypsipyle, the infant's nurse, and asked where they could quench their thirst. Hypsipyle, in a moment of absent-mindedness, set the baby on the ground to point out a nearby spring. With the boy on the ground, a serpent appeared and bit him. Although the heroes quickly killed the snake, it was too late. The boy had died. The heroes held funeral games for the dead child, renaming him Archemoros, or "beginning of doom," treating his death as an inauspicious omen of the expedition's chances of success at Thebes. The story is well attested in ancient sources, with references in the poetry of Simonides and Bacchylides and in one of the lost plays of the tragedian Aeschylus. The surviving fragments of Euripides's tragedy *Hypsipyle* retell the story as well.[2]

A less popular tradition held that Heracles founded the Nemean Games in commemoration of killing the Nemean lion, the first of the great hero's labors or *athla*. This is the version offered by the Hellenistic poet Callimachus in an epinician poem that treats, among other things, the origins of the Nemean and Isthmian Games.[3] According to tradition, the games at Nemea became part of the Panhellenic Crown Games circuit in 573 BCE, making it the last of the four Crown Games sites to be designated.[4]

The History of the Sanctuary

During his visit in the second century CE, Pausanias indicated that the Temple of Zeus at Nemea was still worth visiting, even though the roof had caved in and all of the statues had disappeared, including the cult statue of Zeus.[5] The geographer Strabo does not seem to have even bothered visiting Nemea, confessing that he only viewed the area at a distance from the acropolis of Corinth.[6] Although the area around Nemea shows signs of human habitation dating back to the Neolithic age, the sanctuary of Zeus at Nemea hosted the Nemean Games for only a relatively small number of years during the games' existence.[7] For about ninety years, from the time of the games' development into a Panhellenic event (573 BCE) until the early Classical period (about 480 BCE), the festival at Nemea was administered by the small town of Kleonai, situated about five kilometers (roughly three miles) away. In 468 BCE, the city-state of Argos seized control of the games and the privilege of administering them at the sanctuary of Nemea, although Kleonai continued to assert its traditional rights to the games.[8] Eventually, the Argives relocated the Nemean Games to Argos, about fifteen miles away, probably around the year 420 BCE.

In the words of the principal excavator of the site, Stephen G. Miller, the Nemean Games were a very "moveable festival" since for so many years the actual contests took place away from Nemea at or near the city of Argos.[9] Indeed, the games only took place in the sanctuary at

Nemea for two substantial stretches of time. For about 150 years, from about 573 BCE until 420 BCE, the sanctuary at Nemea was the site of the Panhellenic games, although the Argives assumed control during this time. Archaeology reveals that, sometime between 420 BCE and 410 BCE, the sanctuary at Nemea suffered widespread destruction. These years of the Peloponnesian War featured a considerable amount of Greek warfare in and around this general area, and it seems likely that the sanctuary at Nemea witnessed some of the fighting. During this time, the Temple of Zeus caught fire, and twenty-seven bronze arrowheads recovered near the Shrine of Opheltes suggest that the violence infiltrated the sanctuary itself.[10] Presumably, the damage to the sanctuary persuaded the Argives to relocate the games to Argos.

Around eighty years later, in the 330s BCE, the sanctuary of Nemea received the benefit of a revitalization effort from the Macedonian kings, who had seized control of most of Greece after Philip II and his son Alexander the Great were victorious in the Battle of Chaeronea in 338. The Macedonians' interest in Nemea likely stemmed from the royal house's claimed connections to Heracles, as well as Philip's general recognition of the importance of the Panhellenic sanctuaries. This second period of utilization, a sixty-to-seventy-year span that lasted from about 335 BCE to about 270 BCE, witnessed widespread remodeling and expansion of the sanctuary's buildings. The revival was short lived, however. Archaeology indicates that the games left the sanctuary and were transferred to Argos in about 271 BCE, and there is little evidence for the site of Nemea being used after that.

There was probably one last attempt to bring the Nemean Games back to Nemea. The ancient biographer and Delphic priest Plutarch describes how, in 235 BCE, Aratus of Sicyon, the leader of an alliance of Greek city-states called the Achaean League, attempted to revive the sanctuary at Nemea in opposition to the league's enemies at Argos. After a battle against Argos, Aratus brought the town of Kleonai into the Achaean League and celebrated the Nemean Games "in Kleonai," claiming that this was the more appropriate and ancient location. Stephen G. Miller has argued that these alternative Nemean Games were likely held not at Kleonai itself (about five kilometers away) but instead at Nemea, a sensible explanation for Aratus's claim to be reviving ancient tradition. Archaeological evidence supports this conclusion as well, as some buildings underwent modest remodels during the late third century. Thus, it seems likely that Aratus invited the citizens of Kleonai to reassume their ancient prerogative and to officiate in these alternative games at nearby Nemea.[11]

Argos, however, had other plans, and celebrated its own Nemean Games at Argos, as the Argives had done for decades. With two sets of Nemean Games going on at the same time, Aratus ruthlessly punished anyone caught traveling to the games in Argos. Refusing to observe the legitimacy of the sacred truce that historically had guaranteed safe passage to any of the Crown Games, Aratus ordered that those journeying to Argos's version of the Nemean Games were to be treated as enemies, to be captured and sold into slavery if they were caught trespassing in Achaean League territory.[12]

There is no direct evidence for athletic competitions at Nemea (or Kleonai) from this period of Aratus's control. Plutarch records that, soon after Aratus's alternative Nemean Games, Aratus and his soldiers won a great victory over Argos and its tyrant ruler, and the rivalry between Aratus and Argos seems to have faded away.[13] Archaeology offers no evidence that the games remained at Nemea; it seems that Argos quickly reaffirmed its traditional role of hosting the festival.[14]

Although the Nemean Games crop up in various episodes of Greek and Roman history after 230 BCE, these are typically understood to refer to the Nemean Games that were held at Argos. As Miller points out, a decree at the Nemean Games given by the Roman general Flamininus in 197 BCE could only have taken place at Argos, since the decree was read in a theater, a feature that the ancient sanctuary at Nemea did not possess.[15] One fragmentary inscription discovered at Nemea and dating to the 140s BCE does offer a possibility that the games were returned to Nemea, if only for an instant. Lucius Mummius, a Roman who was commissioned to settle the affairs of Greece, is mentioned in this inscription, as is the phrase "the Contests at Nemea." Although most of the inscription is lost, the inscription was found at Nemea, and the ending for the word "Nemea" seems to indicate that the actual location of Nemea was involved rather than "Nemean" just being used as an adjective.[16] This is hardly compelling evidence, and there is scanty archaeological evidence for a revival at Nemea, although some of the remodeling in a structure called the Xenon might be dated this late. If the Nemean Games were moved back to Nemea in the middle of the second century BCE, they did not leave much of a material record. Thus, the Nemean Games hold the dubious distinction of having been celebrated away from Nemea for the majority of their 800-plus-year existence. Other than the first approximately 150 years and a brief, roughly 65-year resurgence under Macedonian patronage, the Nemean Games were, for the most part, held at Argos, not at Nemea.

At Nemea during the fifth and sixth centuries CE, a farming community built a Christian basilica atop some of the sanctuary's structures. The farmers plowed into the sanctuary's grounds and repurposed some of the stones from the structures, complicating modern attempts to investigate the site's archaeology. A Slavic invasion in about 585 drove out these farmers, and the site was largely abandoned. The site of Nemea attracted visitors from other parts of Europe as early as the eighteenth century, with three still-standing columns of Zeus offering an obvious point of interest. The remnants of the temple amid the heap of rubble caused one writer to declare in 1819 that "Nemea is more characterized by gloom than most of the places I have seen. The splendor of religious pomp, and the busy animation of gymnastic and equestrian exercises, have been succeeded by the dreary vacancy of a death-like solitude."[17]

Some archaeological work at Nemea began in the 1880s as members of the French School of Archaeology undertook small-scale investigations around the Temple of Zeus. The only record of their findings, however, is the publication of the inscriptions that they found.[18] In 1912, the French School cleared the area around the Temple of Zeus and established its basic layout and features. Perceptively, the French archaeologist studying the site noted that the damage to the temple suggested a more deliberate campaign of destruction than the region's endemic earthquakes. Later excavations revealed that the columns of Zeus's temple had toppled over a period of centuries and that extensive looting of the foundations had contributed to the collapses.[19] In 1924, the French School ceded its claims to the study of Nemea to the American School of Classical Studies at Athens. Under the direction of Bert Hodge Hill and Carl W. Blegen, three campaign seasons in the 1920s further revealed the Temple of Zeus at Nemea, but the drawings and photographs from these excavations were not finally published until 1966.[20] Aside from these three excavation seasons in the 1920s, the site remained largely uninvestigated until the 1970s. Led by Dr. Stephen G. Miller of the University of California at Berkeley, archaeologists conducted large-scale excavations during the 1970s and 1980s, routinely publishing their season reports in the journal *Hesperia*, a publication of the American School of Classical

Studies at Athens. In addition, final published reports have been disseminated in four volumes entitled *Excavations at Nemea*, with the most recent appearing in 2018.

The Temple of Zeus at Nemea

The earliest Temple of Zeus was constructed in the early sixth century BCE, at around the same time that the Nemean Games were organized into a Panhellenic event. The size of this earlier temple is unclear since the later, fourth-century-BCE temple sat atop this structure. The earlier temple was almost completely destroyed in the upheavals of the late fifth century BCE, a violent episode evidenced by the thick ash deposits, melted bronze, and large quantities of arrowheads recovered by excavators.[21]

Measuring about forty-two meters long and twenty meters wide, the fourth-century-BCE Temple of Zeus at Nemea had a number of unique or unconventional attributes. For instance, its layout included three different architectural orders—Doric columns in the exterior peristyle, Corinthian columns in the interior colonnade, and Ionic columns along the cella's second story. Strikingly, the finished temple possessed no sculpted metopes and featured an unusual ratio of columns—the columns were six by twelve instead of being in the Classical period's preferred ratio of six to thirteen.

Although the fourth-century-BCE temple was largely unadorned, it did contain an *adyton*, an off-limits area or "holy of holies" that descended nearly two meters into the temple's foundation from an opening with a staircase presumably placed behind the cult statue. The nature of an *adyton* in an ancient Greek temple remains unclear, although the famous oracle at Delphi was seated in the *adyton* in the Temple of Apollo located there. Miller has cautioned against making a connection between the *adyton*, oracles, and the seer Amphiaraos—one of the seven heroes from the Opheltes myth—but the possibility is appealing.[22] There is no written evidence of an oracle at Nemea, nor is there any indication of what uses the *adyton* might have had.

All traces of the cult statue of Zeus that was housed in this fourth-century-BCE temple have completely disappeared, and it was probably moved along with the Nemean Games to Argos. In the second century CE, Pausanias indicated that he had seen a bronze statue of Zeus at the sanctuary of Nemean Zeus at Argos, and this statue—attributed

The Temple of Zeus at Nemea. Author's photograph.

by Pausanias to the well-known sculptor Lysippos of Sicyon—is a strong candidate to have been originally situated at Nemea during the years of the Macedonian revival.[23]

With three columns having remained upright throughout the long centuries, early excavators at Nemea had no trouble identifying the Temple of Zeus. This was the focus of 1920s archaeological investigations. In 1966, a report on the Temple of Zeus at Nemea was published, but the rest of the sanctuary lay mostly undisturbed.[24] Painstaking archaeological work in the 1980s recorded the location and shape of the surviving pieces of the temple, allowing several columns to be restored and reerected in the early 2000s.

The "Sacred Square"

The area around the Temple of Zeus at Nemea, dubbed by its excavators the "Sacred Square," encompassed several monuments and structures that were connected with the sanctuary.[25] The documentary evidence for these constructions is scanty, and their functions remain unclear and unknown.

About 30 feet east of the temple's entrance lie the remnants of a long altar connected to the Temple of Zeus, as is typical of Peloponnesian sanctuaries. The altar measured over 125 feet in length and ran basically north–south, in line with the eastern front of the temple. Many of the blocks were removed from the altar, perhaps in the Christian period, and some of the surviving stones show evidence of farmers' plows passing over them. This unadorned long, low altar at Nemea is similar to the altar at the sanctuary of Poseidon at Isthmia in its considerable length and lack of height. As the excavators noted, it seems to have been "monumental in size" but not "in design or decoration."[26]

South of the Temple of Zeus, within the Sacred Square, several structural foundations have been uncovered, although for the most part, we can only speculate about their functions. The obscurity of these structures is revealed in the generically descriptive names archaeologists have given them. For example, Circular Structure B, located southeast of the Temple of Zeus, featured some type of circular construction with an approximately four-meter (fourteen-foot) diameter. With no evidence of a roof or superstructure, archaeologists have suggested that this series of circular rings could have supported a statue or an altar. On the other side of the Sacred Square, to the west, another circular structure has been uncovered. Dubbed Circular Structure A, this construction was bigger in diameter (six meters, or nearly twenty feet) than Structure B. Pottery sherds in the nearby layers suggest that this building was constructed in the fifth century BCE and that it was destroyed later that century, in conjunction with the devastation that wrecked much of the rest of the sanctuary around the year 420 BCE.

Directly south of the Temple of Zeus, there is a large open area with no structural remains. If perishable dedications or impermanent offerings once adorned this spot, there is no surviving indication. There is, however, evidence of a grove of ancient cypress trees there, corroborating Pausanias's eyewitness statement that such trees were found around the Temple of Zeus at Nemea.[27] Indeed, a "sacred grove" at Nemea is attested in the poetry of Pindar and Euripides as a spot of mourning for the child Opheltes.[28]

The Oikoi

To the south of the Temple of Zeus and the open area that once held cypress trees, excavations have revealed a series of nine buildings, conventionally dubbed *oikoi*, or houses, that defy easy interpretation. Though they were noticed by excavators in the 1920s and 1960s, it was not until the 1970s that the entire row of buildings was uncovered. As with the treasuries at Olympia, the constructions are linear in nature and situated at the edge of sacred space. However, unlike at Olympia, there is no evidence that these buildings were used as treasuries or depositories for dedications to the gods. Indeed, the buildings are much larger than a typical treasury at Olympia or Delphi, and excavators recovered no evidence of valuable or dedicatory offerings.

One of the earliest of these buildings, Oikos 8, at one time featured a bronze-sculpting workshop. The proximity of the furnace and workshop to the Temple of Zeus mirrors a similar arrangement at Isthmia, where bronze statues and offerings could be sculpted and cast on-site. The construction of some of the *oikoi* has been dated to the first half of the fifth century BCE. They seem to have been either destroyed or remodeled by the late fourth century BCE. As with much of the rest of the sanctuary, the *oikoi* fell out of use by the middle of the third century BCE.[29] The buildings were dubbed "houses" because of the domestic nature of their material remains. Some of the buildings featured cooking items and hearths, and one of them contained a well. Nevertheless, these were not full-time residences, as indicated by their modest size and the relative paucity of their stratigraphic deposits. Rather, these buildings seem to have been connected to the sanctuary of Zeus in some official capacity, and a few of the recovered artifacts bear inscriptions indicating that they belonged to Zeus. It has been suggested that these *oikoi*, then, acted as the official quarters of the judges and priests who administered the site and the games to Zeus.[30]

The Xenon

At a size of over eighty-five meters long and almost twenty meters wide, the Xenon is the largest roofed structure yet discovered at Nemea—larger in area even than the Temple of Zeus. Based on this size, the structure presumably held multiple roles at Nemea, and archaeologists are still trying to determine what the building was used for.

Located just south of the *oikoi*, the Xenon was also the site of the later Christian basilica, making archaeological work on the building more problematic. Three seasons of modest excavations in the 1920s led Carl W. Blegen to label this structure a gymnasium, but subsequent investigations have revealed that the building had a variety of uses. In the 1960s, Charles K. Williams II discovered in this building the kiln that had produced the roof tiles used for the Temple of Zeus.[31] Additional excavations have unearthed the ancient road that ran along the building's southern side and presumably demarcated the boundary of the sanctuary. A substantial amount of the building remains underneath the remains of the Christian basilica.

The original Xenon building was divided in half, from east to west, by a wall that ran its entire length. North–south walls divided the interior space into fourteen rooms. Many of the remaining foundation stones appear to have been repurposed or recycled material, presumably from the older, Archaic-period sanctuary that was destroyed around 420 BCE. Included in these recycled materials is a block of stone with a groove running along it, suggesting a piece of the original stadium's starting line.[32] Enough roof tiles have survived for archaeologists to calculate the slope of the building's roof (around eleven degrees), which indicates that at least part of the Xenon was two stories in height. Lynn Kraynak has suggested that the second story sat on the northern portion of the building for architectural reasons, as well as to maximize winter sunshine and summer shade.[33]

Altogether, the Xenon was in use for a relatively short amount of time, as is the case with the rest of the sanctuary. The kiln that fired the tiles of the Temple of Zeus stratigraphically predates the Xenon and offers a clue to dating the Xenon's construction. Since the Temple of Zeus was completed in the 320s BCE, the kiln's use was discontinued sometime after this and the Xenon constructed afterward on the site. The Xenon, like the rest of the sanctuary, was largely abandoned around 270 BCE, giving us a roughly fifty-year window for the building's construction and use. At some later point, a shabby, halfhearted remodeling effort was begun, with poor results. Perhaps this tepid renovation can be connected to the attempted revival of the games at Nemea by Aratus of Sicyon during the late third century BCE.[34]

Although the Xenon was originally identified by modern excavators as a gymnasium, this interpretation has been discarded because of space constraints. There simply is no room next to the Xenon for a stade-length running track, something necessary for a gymnasium—especially a gymnasium located at the site of one of the Crown Games. Subsequent excavations in the Xenon uncovered basic domestic pottery used for eating, drinking, and cooking. Unearthed lamps suggest that the Xenon was sometimes used after dark. These implements imply the presence of banqueting and feasting as at Olympia, although on a more muted and modest scale. It seems likely that the building's rooms had a variety of uses, perhaps as a complement to the *oikoi* just to the north, which would have either been destroyed or undergoing remodeling at the same time as the Xenon's construction.

The Bath

The Bath at Nemea was initially discovered and explored at the same time as the Xenon, in the 1920s. Blocks from the structure protruding into the banks of the nearby Nemea River led to its discovery, although excavations did not begin in earnest until the 1980s. The preservation of the Bath, which measures about thirty-six meters by about twenty meters, is quite poor, owing in part to early Christians' practice of using the area for interring their dead.

The Bath structure itself was divided into two sections. The eastern part apparently contained four columns since four square column bases are easily identified. Although a Doric capital was discovered in the western part of the building, no other trace of the columns has survived. The western half of the building contained four areas. One was a large open area in the northwest quadrant. The southwest section contained the other three areas. Two of these areas featured tubs and basins. The third, central area featured a pool that could have been up to 1¼ meters deep, judging from the height of the filling pipe. All three sections could have been used for bathing, with water being channeled in from a nearby spring or from the Nemea River and stored in reservoirs adjoining the structure. Presumably, patrons used the northern section of the West Room to undress, and from there they descended into either of the tub rooms to wash at the basins. The final step would have been a soak in the central pool. Although there is evidence that the Bath was built atop existing structures, nothing is known about their nature. Very little material evidence survives that could suggest a construction date for the Bath, but masons' marks on some of the foundation blocks and the few recovered pottery fragments suggest a date in the late fourth century BCE, which is consistent with the widespread revitalization that took place throughout the sanctuary at that time.

The function of the East Room of the Baths remains unclear. Early excavators suggested it was used as a palaestra, but palaestra buildings typically stood next to gymnasium structures during Hellenistic times, and no evidence for a gymnasium is forthcoming at Nemea. In addition, a typical palaestra featured a broad, open courtyard for wrestling training, a difficult possibility considering the room's small size. Until more evidence emerges, we cannot go further than to conclude that this room was connected to activities associated with the Baths. Although elaborate baths were common features of the Roman era, it is notable that the Panhellenic sites of Olympia, Delphi, Nemea, and Isthmia all featured plunge pools for athletes as early as the Hellenistic era.[35] Anyone who has visited Olympia or Nemea in the summer months will easily appreciate the value of a refreshing bath after strenuous exercise there.

The Hero Tomb of Opheltes

Although the Nemean festival honored the god Zeus, the child hero Opheltes remained an important part of the sanctuary and its rituals. Pausanias reports that the grave of Opheltes was encircled by a wall of stones at Nemea, and an ancient or medieval commentator on Pindar's *Nemean* odes states that the judges wore black and the victors' crowns were made of celery in remembrance of the dead baby—black for mourning and celery because of the bed of celery that Hypsipyle had laid him on as she attended to the seven heroes who were marching against Thebes.[36]

In 1979, archaeologists discovered a hero shrine to Opheltes about a hundred meters southwest of the sanctuary of Zeus, and excavations at the site continued sporadically until the early 2000s.[37] The excavation report of the Shrine of Opheltes, published in 2018, indicates that this site maintained an important role for much of Nemea's history as a sanctuary and as a focal point for the Nemean Games. As at Isthmia, Olympia, and Delphi, there is evidence of a human presence at Nemea long before the Archaic period saw the development of the site into a Panhellenic sanctuary. The excavation of the Shrine of Opheltes revealed cooking implements from the late Bronze Age, as well as pottery and an iron sword from the Iron Age (ca. 1100–800 BCE). A fragment of a stone wall that predated the Archaic-period shrine has also been unearthed at the site. Much of the shrine's stratigraphy, however, was disrupted by the changing course of the Nemea River during the Christian era.

Despite the challenges posed by the river's erosion, the archaeology of the shrine reveals that, at some time after 575 BCE, during the same time frame when Nemea was developing into a Panhellenic sanctuary with its attendant festival and games, the area next to the river was reshaped into a large mound of earth approximately forty meters wide at the southern end. This low mound, about 1½ to 2 meters higher than the level ground to the east and west, continued north for at least a hundred meters and formed a boundary between the racetrack to the east and the hippodrome to the west. In all, the trapezoid-shaped mound that marked the shrine proper covered over six hundred square meters, and the northern part extended farther as the boundary embankment between the athletic fields.

The focal point of the Shrine of Opheltes centered on a group of low-lying stones that formed a rectangle along the surface of the enclosure. Jorge Bravo, who wrote the excavation report on the shrine, calls this structure a "crude rectangular monument" that nevertheless represented the most visible component of the Opheltes shrine throughout its long history, remaining visible into the Christian era.[38] Below this monument or structure, archaeology has revealed dense layers of pottery dating from the Archaic to the early Hellenistic period, as well as sacrificial debris, including over sixty-eight hundred fragments of mostly burnt animal bones. Fragments of ceramic drinking vessels suggest libation offerings and ritual drinking on the site, and other pottery vessels, such as oil jars, represent dedicatory offerings. In addition, four stone blocks situated nearby were closely connected to the sacrificial remnants, suggesting a role or function as altars. Another pit discovered in the southwest corner of the shrine was a tree-planting pit. It is tempting to identify the tree on the site as a cypress, consistent with the trees around the Temple of Zeus, but the type of tree that once grew in this pit is undetermined. These remains, then, seem to be the wall of stones and altars mentioned by Pausanias at the spot of Opheltes's tomb. Although the identification of specific components of the hero cult are far from definitive, it is clear that cultic rituals and votive offerings consistent with hero worship took place on the site.

Along with this evidence of a hero cult on the site, archaeologists have unearthed at least two small votive statuettes of a young child within the sanctuary at Nemea, one of bronze and another of terra-cotta.

These, presumably, commemorate Opheltes.[39] Pausanias's description, along with the shrine's location next to the early stadium, indicates that this shrine was closely connected to the athletic contests. As at Olympia and—as we will see—at Isthmia and perhaps at Delphi, the presence of a hero tomb near the site of athletic competition was carefully orchestrated and deliberately arranged. As at Olympia and Isthmia, the tomb connected to the games' etiological origin enjoyed a prominent position next to the original racetrack. Furthermore, it seems that the organizers at Nemea took pains to copy this component from Olympia.

Miller has argued that the layout of the site of the Nemean Games was deliberately modeled after the layout of Olympia, and the similarities between the Pelopion at Olympia and the shrine to Opheltes at Nemea seem clear.[40] Although the material remains excavated from the Shrine of Opheltes trail off around the year 270 BCE—the time of the general abandonment of the sanctuary—the basic structures of the shrine remained visible for hundreds of years, at least until the visit of Pausanias in the second century CE. Bravo summarizes the shrine and its role at Nemea by writing that the Shrine of Opheltes "burned briefly, but it burned bright" as the construction of the shrine and the institution of the Nemean Games seem to have coincided.[41] While the Nemean Games honored Zeus, the role of Opheltes at Nemea was prominent as well.

The Early Stadium

The earliest stadium at Nemea was adjacent to the tomb of Opheltes, consistent with the placement of the early stadiums at Olympia and Isthmia. Directly to the east of the tomb's mound, excavators discovered a white clay layer and at least five starting blocks from the earliest stadium, some of which included lane "numbers" to indicate runners' lanes. These characters appear to be consistent with letterforms of late Archaic or early Classical date.[42] Directly to the west of the Ophelteion, Miller identified sixth-to-fifth-century evidence for the hippodrome, including wheel grooves from chariots. Thus, the shrine to Opheltes, in addition to commemorating the hero for whom the games were founded, enjoyed an important vantage point between the two racecourses in the sixth century BCE. The elongated mound served as a barrier between the stadium and the hippodrome, all of which were oriented in the same north–south direction. As Miller conjectures, spectators seated atop the shrine's raised mound could have enjoyed watching athletic competitions in both locations. Eventually, as at Olympia and Isthmia, the site of the stadium was moved away from its original location near the sanctuary to a locale that could support a greater number of spectators.[43]

The Hellenistic Stadium

The Early Hellenistic Stadium at Nemea was built about 450 meters southeast of the Temple of Zeus, where it took advantage of the natural contours of the surrounding hillsides to provide seating for the games' spectators. Although it was tentatively identified as early as 1806, the small-scale excavations of 1925 and 1926 confirmed the stadium's site. While the southern end of the stadium nestled snugly into the contours of the hillside, the northern end of the stadium required a considerable amount of fill and retention to make the ground level to the requisite length. Astonishingly, a retaining wall for the northern end was never built, and much of that end of the stadium has since eroded away. Thus, when excavators began to work on the stadium, they had to remove over seven meters of silt from the southern end, where it abutted the hillside, while the northern end had dropped more than three meters below the projected level of the track's surface. This has prevented a full-scale excavation or restoration of the stadium's original length.

In addition to these disadvantages, the site is rather far from a suitable source of water for the athletes and the spectators. To address this concern, ancient engineers devised an elaborate piping system, some of it discovered in situ by excavators, that brought water to the stadium from the east, covering a distance of at least five hundred meters. Arriving at the stadium, water flowed into a series of basins and then through a channel to basins at either end of the starting line. Presumably, the basins were intended to provide drinking water for the athletes and spectators and for use in preparing the surface of the track.

It is difficult to imagine today how spectators could have crowded into the steeply sloped embankments to watch the athletes compete. It seems likely that the slopes were more gradual in antiquity, and there is some suggestion that temporary seating was available, perhaps only for the judges. Miller has suggested a moderate estimate of around thirty thousand spectators being able to fit into the stadium's spectating areas, although there is no way to know if that many spectators ever actually attended the games.[44]

As we will see was also the case with the stadium at Isthmia, the curved southern end of the stadium at Nemea featured an elaborate starting mechanism developed to give a fair start to those racing in the Nemean Games. A semicircular construction, called a *balbis*, offered a spot for an official to stand and work the mechanism in. The *hysplex* was an apparatus of twisted sinews and vertical wooden posts that acted as gates to keep the runners at the starting point and to ensure that they were evenly spaced along the starting line. When the signal was given, the official standing at the edge of the *balbis* engaged the *hysplex*, causing the cords to pull tight, dropping the gates and sending the runners to chase Nemean glory. The modern reconstruction of the *hysplex* apparatus at Nemea has worked well in starting races for the New Nemean Games (first held in 1996).

Over 150 pre-Christian-era coins have been recovered from the stadium surface, the embankments where the spectators sat, and the adjoining "locker-room" building (called the *apodyterion*). Of these coins, none were discovered in the tunnel (where athletes would have walked and waited in the nude), and only 6 came from the *apodyterion* area. It seems that the coins were mostly dropped or left behind by spectators at the Nemean Games, offering a rare clue about the makeup of the crowd. Unsurprisingly, the majority (75 percent) of the coins found in the stadium came from mints in the nearby Peloponnesian cities of Argos, Corinth, Phlious, Kleonai, and Sicyon. Although there are a few coins from far-off spots such as Thessaly and Crete, the high concentration of local coinage suggests that the majority of the audience came from nearby communities, within a day's walk or so. Interestingly, the distribution of the coins on the stadium's slopes suggests that the people tended to cluster in habitual or traditional spots associated with their hometowns. The coins from Argos were found concentrated around the judges' stand. An adjacent area produced a high concentration of coins from Kleonai. Sicyon's coins were more scattered but also more numerous, concentrating in the area between the tunnel and the curve of the hillside, and next to them was a site heavy with Corinthian coins.[45] This interpretation of the numismatic evidence offers a glimpse of the crowds that came to Nemea to watch the athletic contests in the stadium. It is not difficult to imagine groups from the local communities staking out their traditional sitting spots, perhaps as they looked for shade from the hot sun or enjoyed a snack between competitions. As the crowd congregated along the steep hillside that surrounded three sides of the stadium, they would have trained their eyes on the athletes' entrance, waiting for a local hero or a renowned champion to make a dramatic entrance through the vaulted tunnel that connected the stadium to the "locker room."

The Stadium Entrance

One of the most striking features of the Hellenistic Stadium at Nemea was the vaulted passageway that served as the athletes' entrance and exit to the stadium. When the tunnel was discovered in 1978, both ends of it had been completely filled in with silted earth, although the interior of the tunnel was not completely filled. Restored and strengthened today, the vault measures more than thirty-six meters in length, and in the center, the height rises to 3¼ meters. Numerous graffiti line the stone courses of the vaults, some of which offer an intimate glimpse into the minds of the athletes who competed at Nemea.

Stephen G. Miller has published fifty-seven different tunnel graffiti, found on thirty-five different blocks. The letter sizes and forms are typically irregular, as we might expect of a hastily scratched name or message, and they are grouped toward the eastern end of the tunnel—that is, toward the entrance into the stadium. It is not difficult to imagine athletes waiting in the tunnel for their names or events to be called, whiling away the time by scratching their names into the tunnel walls with a strigil or some other improvised stylus. Most of the graffiti are single names such as Telestas, Polyxenos, Akrotatos, and Andreas. A few of the names have *kalos* (meaning "beautiful" or "handsome") appended, presumably the work of an admirer. One graffito declares, "I win!" Another almost captures a conversation, where the phrase "*Akrotatos kalos*" is punctuated by another graffito, written in another hand, that translates to "to the one who wrote it"—that is, not everyone considers Akrotatos to be quite so *kalos*. Astonishingly, another graffito of the name Akrotatos occurs elsewhere in the tunnel; presumably this autograph was scratched by the athlete's own hand. As Miller has pointed out, this name is quite rare in antiquity, and the few instances of it are associated with Sparta in the third century BCE, a time consistent with the stadium's use before the Nemean Games again relocated to Argos. We can construct a possible and plausible scenario where Akrotatos scratched his own name, another watching him commented on his beauty, and a third character disagreed with the admirer's estimation. Although highly conjectural, this scenario offers a glimpse of the athletes and their world, something rarely obtained from the ruins of the Crown Games locales.[46]

At the western end of the tunnel, the end closer to the sanctuary of Zeus and farther from the stadium, stood a sizeable building, measuring about sixteen meters by thirty meters, that connected to the entrance tunnel. Very few of the building's foundation blocks have survived, having presumably been repurposed in later years. This building, called the *apodyterion*, featured nine Doric columns arranged in a U formation, with an open courtyard and roofed interior. With a channel cut through the bedrock connecting it to the stadium tunnel, it is clear that the *apodyterion* was constructed in tandem with the tunnel. Since this building gave exclusive access to the entrance tunnel, presumably only athletes, coaches, priests, and other officials of the games had access to this building. Possibilities for this building's uses include a dressing/undressing room, warm-up rooms, and judging rooms, and visitors typically refer to it as a "locker room" of some sort.[47]

When the Nemean Games left Nemea for good, around 270 BCE, perhaps with the exception a brief resurgence under Aratus, the sanctuary at Nemea entered a long period of neglect and decline. It seems likely that some of the late fourth-century-BCE building program that prompted the construction of the new stadium and the renovation of the sanctuary was unfinished when the games left and that it was never completed. Indeed, retaining walls at the north end of the stadium were never built, dooming the track to erosion. Very few pottery fragments dating later than 270 BCE have been discovered in the area, and of the 152 coins discovered around the stadium, only 3 coins, from the Roman era, can be dated after 270 BCE. In addition, excavators discovered in the tunnel entrance over twenty fragments of bronze statuary that had been broken sometime before the entrance collapsed, an event reckoned to have occurred around the first century BCE. It seems that the stadium of Nemea at that time was largely disused, with the only discernible activity coming from an intrepid looter who broke down some bronze statues and carted away the pieces for reuse, leaving behind the small fragments in the tunnel entrance.[48]

Despite the limited number of years that the sanctuary of Zeus at Nemea actually hosted the Nemean Games and the paucity and poverty of the material record, the excavations at Nemea provide us with some of the most personal evidence about the ancient Crown Games. The coins in the stadium and the graffiti in the stadium tunnel offer a valuable glimpse into the world of the athletes and spectators who attended the Crown Games. The small bronze coins that slipped unnoticed to the sloped ground of the stadium embankment and the hand-scratched graffiti, etched moments before a thrilling competition by presumably excited and anxious athletes, offer a human connection to the Crown Games that is difficult to capture at the other sites. Although in some ways the material record at Nemea is much poorer than at the other Crown Games sites, it also offers a unique richness and texture for understanding the games. Now that we've visited Olympia and Nemea, the next stop in our Crown Games circuit is the Isthmus of Corinth, where the festival to Poseidon was celebrated every two years.

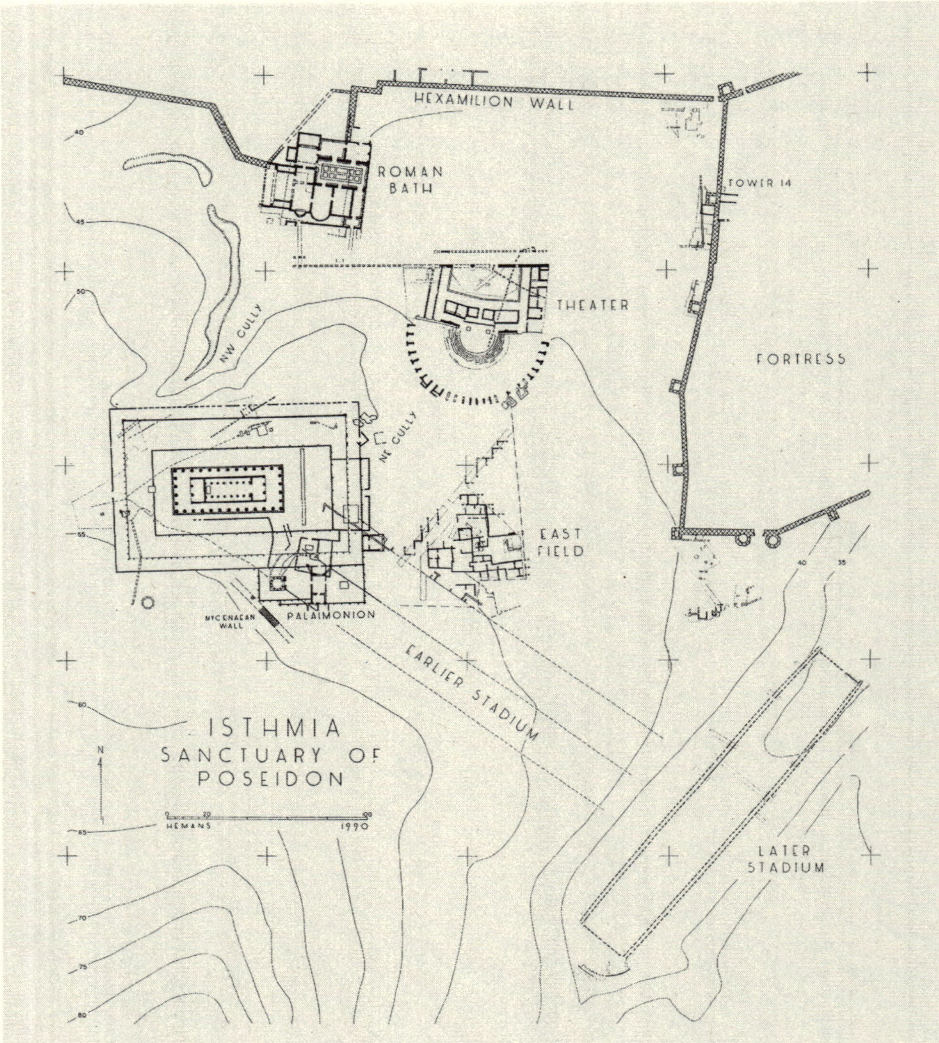

Site plan of ancient Isthmia. From Elizabeth R. Gebhard and Frederick P. Hemans, "University of Chicago Excavations at Isthmia: II," Hesperia 67 (1998): 2, fig. 1. Image courtesy of the Trustees of the American School of Classical Studies at Athens.

CHAPTER 4

Isthmia and the Isthmian Games

Honor him, who obtained the Dorian celery
at the Isthmian glen.

—PINDAR, *ISTHMIAN* 8.63–64

Corinth and the Sanctuary of Isthmia

The Isthmus of Corinth, that narrow spit of land connecting the Peloponnese to the rest of mainland Greece, has long been recognized as an important location for trade and defense. As the meeting place of sea routes to both Asia and Italy, the isthmus acted as a crossroads for sea travel in the ancient world, and the biennial Isthmian Games were sacred to Poseidon, the god of the sea. The traditional date for the foundation of the Isthmian Games is 582 or 580 BCE.[1] Located only about ten kilometers away from Isthmia, the nearest major city-state, Corinth, took advantage of its location on the isthmus to develop as a maritime power during ancient Greece's Classical period (480–323 BCE). Corinth also benefited from the Isthmian Games, which brought crowds of people to the area.[2] During the Hellenistic period (323–31 BCE), the Acrocorinth or the acropolis of Corinth, played a prominent role as one of the vaunted "three fetters" of Greece, vital strongholds for controlling and protecting the country.[3]

In the third century BCE, the expansive Roman Republic grew increasingly involved in affairs in the Balkan region as Roman shipping ran into Illyrian pirates along the Adriatic coastline. After the First Illyrian War ended in 228 BCE with Roman shipping lanes secured, the Romans remained involved in the Greek mainland. The ancient historian Polybius informs his readers that soon after settling with the Illyrian pirates, the Roman government sent envoys to Athens and Corinth, and it was at about this time that the Romans began to compete in the Isthmian Games.[4] The Romans would leave an indelible mark on the Isthmian Games. Just over thirty years after this war concluded, after Rome had defeated the Macedonian king Philip V in 197 BCE, it was at the Isthmian Games in 196 BCE that the Roman commander Titus Quinctius Flamininus proclaimed "freedom for the Greeks," an announcement that provoked wild rejoicing and celebrating among the Greeks.[5]

In 146 BCE, when the Greek Achaean League undertook a "hopeless, and hysterical" war against the Romans, a Roman commander named Lucius Mummius marched to Corinth, utterly destroyed the city, and ravaged the nearby sanctuary at Isthmia.[6] Corinth was not rebuilt for over a hundred years, until Julius Caesar gave the command in 44 BCE to resettle on the site. Although the sanctuary at Isthmia was damaged or destroyed along with Corinth in 146, Pausanias indicates that the Isthmian Games were not suspended, having been transferred to the nearby city of Sicyon. When Corinth was rebuilt under the Romans, the sanctuary at Isthmia was revived, and the Isthmian Games eventually returned to their traditional site on the isthmus, although not until the forties CE.[7]

Because of its strategic location on the Isthmus of Corinth, Isthmia maintained military importance well into the Middle Ages. In the early fifth century CE, a nearly six-mile wall called the Hexamilion Wall (the word *hexamilion* denotes "six miles") was built to protect the Peloponnese from invaders from the north, and a nearby fortress enjoyed a strong strategic location. Many of the dressed stones from the ancient sanctuary of Poseidon were incorporated into these fortifications and wall. This complex history makes uncovering Isthmia particularly challenging for archaeologists, as well as visitors who are looking to explore the origins and features of the Panhellenic competitions that were held on the site.

The Foundation Myth

Although, as Pausanias states, "the isthmus belong[ed] to Poseidon" and the Isthmian Games honored the god of the sea, as we saw at Nemea, the foundation myth for the games commemorated the death of a child.[8]

While there are some variations, the most common version of the Isthmian mythic tradition tells how Ino, the daughter of Cadmus (the founder of Thebes in central Greece), in a fit of madness jumped with her son Melikertes into the sea. Although Ino was transformed into a sea nymph named Leukothea, the boy met a sadder fate: he drowned. The child's name was changed to Palaimon, and a dolphin gently carried the boy's body to shore at Isthmia. The myth relates that Sisyphus, who ruled the land around Corinth, buried the body and instituted the Isthmian Games in Palaimon's honor.[9]

Although the majority of literary references to the foundation of the Isthmian Games date from the Roman era, this can be attributed to the fragmentary nature of the evidence as well as a renewed focus on the cult of Palaimon after the refounding of Corinth in 44 BCE. Although less complete than the Roman-period sources, earlier literary accounts secure Palaimon's presence at Isthmia long before the Roman period. A fragment of Pindar from the fifth century BCE mentions the honors that Sisyphus paid to the dead boy, and a Hellenistic-era fragment of Callimachus alludes to the games for the "brother of Learkos"—that is, Melikertes/Palaimon.[10] These fleeting references are important for establishing the presence of the boy hero at Isthmia before the Roman period and for understanding his connection to the earliest version of the Isthmian Games.

The Sanctuary and Temple of Poseidon

Because the Roman destruction Corinth was so complete and the site of Isthmia left deserted for perhaps up to 150 years, the description offered by Pausanias in the second century CE refers to the rebuilt Roman version of the sanctuary that he viewed during his visit. Modern archaeological excavations, however, have unearthed details of the site's Archaic-period origins and early buildings. Although earlier travelers in the modern era had readily identified the remnants of the site's stadium and theater, systematic archaeological excavations at Isthmia began only in 1952 under the direction Oscar Broneer and the University of Chicago.[11] These excavations uncovered the foundations of a temple dedicated to Poseidon, in addition to other cult sites.

Although archaeologists uncovered Bronze Age pottery from the Late Helladic period at Isthmia, there is no evidence for any Bronze Age religious cult or ritual activity, and the excavators determined that these pottery sherds were likely connected to a "small-scale settlement."[12] There is little evidence for any cult dedicated to Poseidon at Isthmia before the end of the eighth century BCE, but around the year 700 BCE, the sanctuary to Poseidon was organized.[13] As we saw at Olympia, the site at Isthmia was sacred to the gods long before the introduction of athletic contests. And, again similar to what the archaeological record at Olympia shows, the sanctuary at Isthmia received increased attention around the end of the eighth century.

Around this time, 700 BCE, the Archaic temple to Poseidon was built—a large structure that measured over forty meters long. Presumably, it was the people of Corinth who oversaw the construction of this temple since the style and size of the temple at Isthmia corresponded closely to a similar contemporaneous construction at Corinth.[14] This temple stood on the site of Isthmia when the Isthmian Games were organized on a Panhellenic scale around the year 580 BCE. About a hundred years later, sometime in the early fifth century BCE (Broneer suggested between the years 480 BCE and 470 BCE), this Archaic-period temple was extensively damaged or destroyed by fire. The fire was particularly intense and destructive, resulting in many of the bronze dedications—including over a hundred helmets—melting into undistinguishable lumps.[15]

The Temple of Poseidon did not remain in ruins for long: within a few years, a new Classical-period temple rose on the same spot. This new temple was similar in size and shape to the Temple of Zeus at Olympia, employing the traditional six-by-thirteen column ratio for its layout. In the early fourth century BCE, around the year 390 BCE, this version of the temple suffered damage from a fire, but the damage was not nearly as extensive as that suffered in the preceding century. The temple was not destroyed: rather, it was repaired and remodeled. It was this Classical-period temple that remained on the site for more than seven hundred years, presumably suffering privations after the abandonment of the sanctuary in 146 BCE and then experiencing a revitalization along with the rest of the sanctuary under Roman supervision during the first century CE. In the fifth century CE, after the end of the Isthmian Games and the Roman imperial edict forbidding pagan worship, the Temple of Poseidon was dismantled and its materials used to build the Hexamilion Wall and fortifications just a few meters to the north.

Because of the destruction of the Archaic-period temple by fire and the privations of the Roman sack of Corinth, many of the material remains of the temple, including its dedications and decorations, have disappeared. Although literary sources claim that the Roman commander Lucius Mummius restored the sanctuary at the Isthmus soon after the destruction of Corinth in 146 BCE, the archaeology suggests a different story. It seems that the site became largely neglected. Indeed, it is easy to believe that, without the city of Corinth to maintain the buildings and to administer the biennial festival to Poseidon, the site of Isthmia slipped into ruin. With Isthmia neglected, the people of Sicyon moved the Isthmian Games to their nearby city until Corinth was rebuilt.[16]

Despite the paucity of material remains at the site today, the sources suggest that the sanctuary of Poseidon at Isthmia was at one time rich and lavish and featured expensive dedications and ornate cult statues. The debris recovered from the destruction of the Archaic temple hint at its riches. Since they belonged to the gods, the ruined dedications were buried on-site after the fire, and modern excavations have turned up silver coins, bronze figurines, and a miniature gold bull.[17] The Classical-period sanctuary was undoubtedly rich as well, although its contents seem to have largely disappeared in wake of the Roman conquest. After the refounding of Corinth and the eventual restoration of the Isthmian Games to Isthmia in the forties CE, the site became rich once again, as attested by the description of Pausanias and the largesse of a rich Roman named Herodes Atticus. In the second century CE, Pausanias described four gilded horses with ivory hooves pulling a chariot that carried Poseidon and Amphitrite his queen, attended by golden Tritons and a chryselephantine statue of Palaimon atop a dophin.[18] The Classical-period temple, with several rounds of renovations (including a renovation of the central cella that merged its two aisles into one), stood until the fifth century CE when it was dismantled to provide material for the fortification of the Isthmus.[19]

The Altar

Although there is no evidence for an altar during the Archaic period, there is evidence of copious animal sacrifices in a large area directly to the east of the Temple of Poseidon, where altars traditionally stood in relation to temples. Archaic-period renovations to this portion of the site raised the level of the ground, allowing for a large area to be dedicated to sacrificial offerings. Large amounts of ash and residue from sacrificial victims were recovered from an area forty meters long and twenty meters wide, indicating a large sacrificial area connected to the temple. Interestingly, excavations of the Archaic level of this sacrificial area revealed heaps of numerous pebbles about the size of a hen's egg that were clearly placed in the area deliberately, presumably as part of the sacrificial ritual. Broneer speculates that casting pebbles at the animals allowed the worshippers to ritually participate in the sacrifice by throwing their rocks at the designated victims.[20] Even after a long altar of some forty meters in length (but less than two meters wide) was constructed during the Classical period, the stone-throwing ritual persisted, as more pebbles emerged directly in front of the altar's foundation on the west side (the temple side) but not on the east, supporting the idea that the stones were thrown or placed deliberately and in conjunction with the sacrifices at the altar.[21] During the period of neglect after 146 BCE, the altar was removed, and two roads crossed its site, leaving their wheel tracks in its foundation.[22]

The Stadium

As noted above, the Archaic Temple of Poseidon dates from around the year 700 BCE, and the earliest phase of the nearby athletic stadium seems to have been constructed about a century later, in conjunction with the development of a Panhellenic athletic festival as one of the Crown Games around the year 580 BCE. Since the immediate vicinity of the temple and sanctuary featured no obvious long flat area for an improvised racetrack, this early stadium at Isthmia required its builders to exert a considerable amount of effort to extend and level the track to a suitable length. The construction of this early stadium, which excavator Elizabeth R. Gebhard characterized as a "massive earth-moving project," resulted in a configuration that closely connected the stadium to the altar of Poseidon.[23] Indeed, the entrance to the stadium lay only about ten meters from the edges of both the temple and the altar. This extensive building project indicates an important feature of Archaic-period competitions: the running track needed to be closely connected to the sanctuary. A suitable stretch of flat terrain was available just a short distance from the site (in fact, this is where the later stadium was situated), but it was important for the organizers of the early games to connect the athletic site closely to the sanctuary.

In 1955, Broneer uncovered the starting line for this early racetrack. Its most notable feature was a triangular series of grooves with a pit, about a meter deep, in which an official could stand holding cords that passed through the grooves. Earlier, we encountered another version of this mechanism in the Hellenistic Stadium at Nemea. The version of the *hysplex* at Isthmia ran cords through grooves cut into the stadium's stone surface, which threaded their way back to the starting official who stood in the starter's pit controlling all of the cords. The cords were connected to sixteen gates that separated the runners at the starting line with posts and crossbars. As at Nemea, at the signal the race official would pull all of the cords at once, release the sixteen crossbars, and send the racers on their way. Broneer speculates that this mechanism must have been cumbersome, and later versions of the stadium at Isthmia replaced it with a grooved starting line, absent the gates.[24] The improved version of the *hysplex* discovered at Nemea did not feature a pit for the race starter; instead, the cords to the runners' gates were already pulled taut, and a small motion by a race official could release the tension and start the race. At the northern corner of the first stadium at Isthmia, a ramp connected the athletic grounds to the sanctuary of Poseidon near the long altar, and presumably this was the entrance used by athletes as they descended from the sanctuary toward the starting line during the Archaic period.

The Later Stadium

Eventually, as at Olympia, Nemea, and presumably (as we will see) Delphi, the stadium's location at Isthmia was shifted. It seems likely that the new stadium was built to accommodate increased numbers of pilgrims and spectators, and by Pausanias's time in the second century CE, around seven hundred years after the construction of the original, the stadium had been moved about two hundred meters to the southeast and its orientation changed to align with the more convenient topography of a stream bed and hillsides for spectators. It is uncertain exactly when the stadium's location was shifted, but Broneer suggested that such a costly undertaking must have corresponded with some important event at Corinth, such as the ambitious building program of Philip and Alexander in the mid-fourth century BCE.[25] The later stadium remains largely unexcavated, although Broneer sank several trenches between 1960 and 1962. These trenches revealed the general layout of the stadium, a combination of Greek and Roman handiwork, and an extensive water-channeling network that ended in a reservoir to provide drinking water for the athletes and spectators. The basins of this reservoir featured cleverly painted fish intended to create the illusion that they were swimming in the water's depths.[26] Similar to the stadiums at the other Crown Games sites, this later stadium appears to have been constructed with an eye toward accommodating crowds and the spectacle of the Crown Games. But the original, earlier stadium, as at the other Crown Games sites, was much closer to the Temple of Poseidon. This proximity indicates a close connection between the athletic contests and both the temple and the shrine to the hero Palaimon.

The Shrine of Palaimon

The proximity of the earliest stadium to the sanctuary of Poseidon is easily enough established, but identifying the presence of the child hero Melikertes/Palaimon near the stadium and the sanctuary during the Archaic period has proven more difficult.

Although a valuable source, Pausanias's account of the sanctuary of Poseidon at Isthmia describes the sanctuary during his own day—that is, the second century CE—several hundred years after the foundation of the Isthmian Games. A statue group inside the (Roman-era) Temple of Poseidon featured Poseidon and his wife Amphitrite riding in a chariot. Among their entourage was a statue of Palaimon, the boy hero, standing atop a dolphin.[27] Pausanias also reports that the shrine to Palaimon was located close by, just inside the wall of the temple's sacred precinct. This Roman-period shrine featured statues of Poseidon, Leukothea (Palaimon's mother), and the boy himself. In addition, a hidden monument in the shrine's *adyton* was supposed to commemorate the location of Palaimon's body.[28]

The literary accounts of the Palaimon myth found in the works of ancient mythographers such as Apollodorus and Philostratus indicate that the dolphin swam to shore with the boy's body lying across its back. Philostratus's account is quite clear in its explanation that the dolphin straightened its back so as not to disturb the boy's sleep.[29] Perhaps with this component of the myth in mind, Pausanias explicitly notes that the sculpture group featured Palaimon standing "upright" atop the dolphin, implying that he lives on in the company of Poseidon. Despite his being a child with little to recommend him for immortal honors, the images and stories of Palaimon at the sanctuary of Isthmia stressed the notion of continuation after death, and the proximity of the athletic facilities with these images, as at other Crown Games sites, juxtaposed the achievements of living athletes with the commemoration of the dead.

The Roman-era shrine of Palaimon that Pausanias visited lay to the south of the Temple of Poseidon, atop the remains of the older stadium, and was fairly easily identified by the site's twentieth-century excavators. Despite the ancient nature of the Palaimon myth at Isthmia, as indicated by the poetry of Pindar and Callimachus, all of the material remains of this shrine of Palaimon date from the Roman period. Various pits surrounding this shrine contained a considerable amount of votive and ritual material dated from the Roman period—that is, specifically after the first century CE.[30] Broneer suggested that the large number of lamps discovered in these deposits supports ancient descriptions of the nocturnal mystery rites that were observed in the worship of the boy hero.[31] Indeed, the material evidence for the worship of Palaimon at Isthmia is so firmly grounded in the Roman period that John G. Hawthorne argued in 1958 that the institution of this cult at Isthmia actually took place during the Roman Empire![32] Nevertheless, despite Hawthorne's objections, Palaimon was clearly recognized at Isthmia as an important hero figure during the Classical period, and there is evidence for a hero cult at Isthmia during the Archaic period—a cult most probably associated with Palaimon.

Hawthorne overlooked the fragment of Pindar and the reference in Callimachus that connect the story of the dead boy with the games at Isthmia, although they admittedly do not explicitly mention cultic rituals. In addition, an inscribed *halter* (jumping weight) discovered in the debris from the Archaic temple might refer to the boy hero. The inscription, dated by Broneer based on Archaic letter types to around 575 BCE, states that it was dedicated by the winner of the pentathlon. Although the inscription is difficult to decipher, the most persuasive restoration for the second line is to "Inoides," the matronymic term for Palaimon, the son of Ino.[33] As Broneer remarked, the "dedicator would not have offered this tool of his trade to the son of Ino, had he not then been revered by athletes as their protector and giver of victory."[34] Besides these tantalizing glimpses of Palaimon in the Archaic-age sanctuary, it has been suggested that three "foundation stones" found near the site of the sanctuary could be the remnants of an earlier shrine or statue group, and a recovered fragment of an Archaic-period kouros sculpture of a young man might have been connected with the figure of Palaimon.[35]

Finally, the Roman-era shrine to Palaimon conceivably owed its location to the site of an earlier shrine to the boy.[36]

While the Roman-period Palaimonion was located atop and to the west of the earlier Archaic stadium, a series of pits to the east of this original stadium offers some of the most intriguing clues to finding Palaimon at pre-Roman Isthmia. The contents of these pits suggest cultic rites for a hero long before the Roman-period structure covered up the old racetrack. One pit on the East Terrace of the sanctuary, called by excavators Pit A, measured about 1½ by 1¼ meters and was 76 centimeters deep. Pit A was located about 9 meters from the edge of the altar of Poseidon and about 5 meters from the eastern edge of the Archaic stadium. This pit seems to be a viable candidate for a location for offerings to the boy hero.

Pit A, dated by its contents to the Archaic period, contained a considerable amount of debris associated with rituals and offerings. Excavators found ash, eighty-eight burnt animal bones (of which nearly 98 percent were identified as sheep/goat), and over two hundred sherds of pottery, some of which were clearly dedicatory.[37] Elizabeth R. Gebhard, who reexcavated the site in 1989, concluded that the pit appeared to have been connected with cult activity, that it was in use for approximately fifty years, and that it was filled in shortly after the Archaic Temple of Poseidon burned down between 480 BCE and 470 BCE. In addition, the location and construction of Pit A imply that a good deal of care went into establishing and maintaining the site. When it was constructed, the boulders on the south end were deliberately shaped and trimmed off. Evidence also exists for a wooden post that continued to mark the location after the pit was filled in. While the nearby Pits C, D, and E probably had a "more limited use" as receptacles for the sacrificial remnants from the altar of Poseidon, Pit B also contained pottery sherds from the Archaic period and was roughly contemporaneous with Pit A. However, only Pit A appears to have been commemorated with a wooden marker or post after it was filled in.[38]

The contents of Pit A offer some of the most substantial evidence for a hero cult at Isthmia during the Archaic period. Although this pit yielded no specific evidence of worship of Palaimon, it is likely that a hero of some sort was worshiped and commemorated there. Perishable offerings, such as garlands and libations, would have left no archaeological trace. The recovery of a piece of an Attic lecythus, a ceramic vessel associated with grave sites, from this pit also implies that this site was connected with a grave, possibly of a heroic figure.[39]

While hardly conclusive, these discoveries provide at least some circumstantial evidence for an Archaic-period Palaimon cult in the sanctuary, near—indeed, practically within—the early stadium at Isthmia. Although the evidence is tenuous, the suggested location for an Archaic- and Classical-period Palaimon shrine, near the site of the later Roman construction, closely connects the tomb of the boy with the site of the competitions. In addition, Pit A's prominent location, marked with a post and situated at the stadium entrance, would have reminded athletes of the connections between hero cult and the field of competition. While far from conclusive, the archaeological record seems to support a connection between athletic competitions, the sanctuary, and the tomb of a hero, as found at other Crown Games sites during the Archaic period.

The Theater

Although only the indentation of its shape remains, the theater at Isthmia hosted a variety of musical events during the Classical and Roman eras. Literary and epigraphic sources mention musical contests at Isthmia, although few details about these events survive. Inscription evidence indicates that dramas were staged there, presumably (but not certainly) as competitions separate from the Crown Games events. Excavated in the 1950s and 1960s, the theater at Isthmia underwent several phases of building and remodeling, continuing well into the Common Era.[40]

There is no clear-cut evidence of the date of construction for the first, or earliest, phase of the theater at Isthmia. Fragments of pottery found in the silt of the underground drain suggest that the initial construction of the theater took place perhaps around the year 400 BCE, probably predating the fire that damaged the Temple of Poseidon in the early fourth century.[41] Renovations undertaken at the end of the fourth century BCE updated the theater to a more conventional "curvilinear" plan, including twelve rows of permanent seats that would have seated around fifteen hundred people, with room for plenty more on the hillside above.[42] Although there may have been small alterations or updates, the theater remained essentially the same until the middle of the first century of the Common Era, after the games had returned to Isthmia.

In the middle of the first century CE, repairs and alterations to the theater at Isthmia were undertaken in preparation for a visit from the Roman emperor Nero, who competed in the Isthmian Games and who would have used the theater for his musical contests.[43] This renovation, however, did not transform the theater into a Roman-style odeum but remained faithful to the traditional Greek architecture. A hundred years later, around 150 CE, the theater was again rebuilt and expanded. Shortly after, an impressed Pausanias noted that "the theater and the white stone stadium" at Isthmia were "worth seeing."[44] However, as the Roman Empire in the late fourth century closed the pagan cult centers, Isthmia became a source of building material for other constructions, and the theater was dismantled.

The earliest surviving record of an Isthmian musical victor is an inscription found at Athens, dated to the late fourth century BCE, commemorating Nikokles, the son of Aristokles. Nikokles was a *kitharodos*—one who sang while playing the kithara—and the inscription includes the words "*Isthmia Protos*" surrounded by a pine wreath.[45] The use of the word *protos* is unusual, and its meaning, "first," might indicate that Nikokles was the winner of the first ever *kitharodos* contest at Isthmia, or it might just mean that he took first place.

In the early years of the third century BCE, musical performers and actors began to organize themselves into guilds throughout the Greek world. The most prominent of these guilds were the Athenian guild and the Isthmian-Nemean guild.[46] A copy of a now-lost inscription erected at Hermione, Greece, boasted that a man named Pythocles had won as a chorus leader thirteen times at Nemea, Isthmia, and Delphi and at Olympia perhaps three additional times.[47] While it is unclear to what extent the dramatic and musical competitions corresponded to the traditional Crown Games program of gymnastic and equestrian competitions at Isthmia, these events must have been held in the theater.

The Roman Baths and Eastward

In the 1970s, archaeologists at Isthmia discovered and excavated a large bathing complex dating from the Roman period north of the Temple of Poseidon. A large mosaic (ca. eight by twenty meters) adorns the floor of the Roman baths, featuring a Nereid, a Triton, dolphins, and assorted sea life, all consistent with a location dedicated to Poseidon.[48] This second-century-CE structure was built over the top of a Greek-period bathing structure that can be dated to the fourth century BCE. As excavators worked to protect and conserve the monochrome mosaic in the large hall of the Roman baths, they discovered that the baths had been constructed on the remnants of a large swimming pool from the fourth century BCE. This pool, estimated to be about 1.4 meters deep, took up a considerable amount of space, measuring over 900 square meters in all.[49] As we have seen at Olympia and at Nemea, a plunge pool must have been a welcome luxury for the hot and tired athletes.

To the south of the Roman baths (and to the north of the Temple of Poseidon), preliminary archaeological investigations have revealed additional buildings and structures that are as yet unexcavated. Early indications suggest a colonnade, but the proximity to the furnace rooms that heated the baths, a place of heat and ash and soot, probably rules out the possibility of a colonnade belonging to a facility for exercise or athletics.

However, to the east of the Roman baths and the north of the theater, a large open area offers more promising possibilities for an ancient athletic training site. Archaeologists have uncovered evidence that this area once featured a Doric-style stoa, or covered colonnade. Column sections, cornice blocks, and column capitals have been uncovered in the Hexamilion Wall to the north. This stoa probably was in use at the same time as the swimming pool—that is, in the Hellenistic period. There is also evidence of three more buildings here that enclosed a spacious open area—all to the north of the theater and east of the Roman baths. In addition, an elaborate drain system to the north of the theater indicates a desire to keep that open area free of water. In 2016, archaeologists Jon Frey and Timothy Gregory suggested that this enclosed rectangular area, measuring about 175 meters on its north side and around 70 meters on the east and west, was large enough to contain a full-size *xystus*, or covered racing track, (running east–west) equal at least to the length of a stadium, which could have been used by athletes for training before and during the competitions.[50]

The existence of a training facility of this type, featuring a *xystus*, a colonnaded palaestra, and a swimming pool, corresponds to the archaeology of the Crown Games sites at Olympia and Delphi. So far, archaeology has revealed only a pool at Nemea. Although the Roman rebuilding of the second century CE and the construction of the Hexamilion Wall have thoroughly rearranged the site of Isthmia, the suggestion that this part of the sanctuary featured athletic training facilities in line with those of the other Crown Games sites is both logically and archaeologically sound. Further excavation and study are necessary, however, before this hypothesis can be proven.

The Written Accounts

Written records refer to Isthmia, usually in passing, as an advantageous site for addressing large numbers of people from many parts of the Greek world. Its location as a crossroads made it strategically and logistically important and a convenient place for Greeks to meet. Remember, it was at Isthmia that the Greeks commanders met after the decisive and momentous Battle of Salamis had turned the tide in the war against the Persians in 480 BCE. It was there, on the altar of Poseidon, that the commanders cast their ballots for awarding commendations for the battle.[51]

Like Delphi and Olympia, Isthmia might have at one time had some kind of prophetic or oracular function, but the evidence is very sparse. An inscribed statue base of white marble discovered in the area of the Roman shrine of Palaimon features an inscription identifying "Blastos the Seer."[52] The letterforms of the inscription suggest a Roman date. Perhaps this seer was connected to the hidden area within the shrine of Palaimon.[53]

In the early fifth century BCE, the Athenian Aeschylus wrote a tragic play that featured the Isthmian Games. Fewer than a hundred lines of this play, usually called *Isthmiastae*, have survived, making it difficult to reconstruct the play's plot or action conclusively. The play seems to have been set at Isthmia in the context of the Isthmian Games. In the surviving lines, a chorus of satyrs has come to the Temple of Poseidon, and the satyrs are dedicating images of themselves to the god. When confronted by one of the play's characters, probably Dionysus, the chorus is criticized for neglecting its dancing in favor of pursuing the Isthmian crown. There is reason to believe that Aeschylus was familiar with the sanctuary at Isthmia, for the chorus and an unnamed actor speak of iron-working implements in close proximity to the temple used to manufacture athletic equipment. True to Aeschylus's play, excavations of the sanctuary of Poseidon have revealed evidence for a metal foundry within the precinct.[54] Although the surviving fragments of the play reveal frustratingly little about the Isthmian Games themselves, Dionysus's complaint suggests the presence of dramatic competition in conjunction with the athletic festival. In the play, Dionysus complains that the satyrs have abandoned their dramatic craft in favor of athletics even though he has summoned the people of "the Isthmian land" to come to the performance.[55] Although the linkage is tenuous, the fragment suggests some connection between athletic and dramatic performances at Isthmia in the fifth century BCE.

Isthmia's popularity, especially during the Roman era, seems to have engendered a certain amount of rivalry with Olympia and its grand festival to Zeus. Pausanias indicates that athletes from Elis (the city-state responsible for administering the Olympian Games) refused to participate in the Isthmian festival. Although he offers several possible explanations, he ultimately argues that their refusal stems from mythic times. The story goes that Heracles ambushed and killed two Eleans as they made their way to the Isthmian Games. Since Corinth had already proclaimed the peace of the Isthmian Games at the time of the attack, the people of Elis demanded retribution from Heracles. Unsuccessful at receiving recompense, the mother of the dead men placed "curses" on her own people of Elis to prevent them ever after from entering the Isthmian Games.[56] Although this story is mythic, it nevertheless underscores the potential rivalry between the city-states of Elis and Corinth as each sought to capitalize on its administration of a Crown Games festival to augment its own civic identity and prestige. Regardless of the origins of the feud, Pausanias emphasizes this story enough times to indicate that he took seriously the Elean refusal to compete at Isthmia. Of the admittedly few athletic victors at the Isthmus whose names and origins we know today, none of them were from Elis.

The Isthmian Crown

The reward for victory in the Isthmian Games varied between a crown of pine and a crown of wild celery or parsley (*selinon* in ancient Greek). According to the literary sources, a crown of pine was awarded because the dead child Melikertes was placed on a litter of pine boughs.[57] We know the pine crowns were in use during the time of Aeschylus—that is, the early fifth century BCE—since his play *Isthmiastae* mentions that victors in the Isthmian Games are crowned with branches of pine.[58] However, at some point in the middle of the fifth century BCE, Isthmia's victory crown was changed to celery out of rivalry with the Nemean Games. This change is apparent in the victory odes of Pindar, who composed his verses shortly after Aeschylus, during the second quarter of the fifth century. *Olympian* 13 commends the victories of Xenophon of

Corinth and includes mention of the parsley crowns he won at Isthmia. *Nemean* 4 and two *Isthmian* odes also use the word *selinon* to indicate victory at Isthmia.[59] Later, as Plutarch informs his readers, the pine crown was reintroduced at Isthmia for victors in the contests.

The Isthmian Festival

The athletic competitions at Isthmia followed, for the most part, the Olympian program.

A speech, possibly spurious, attributed to the first-to-second-century-CE orator Dio Chrysostom, offers an explanation that the first Isthmian Games were contests among heroes, many of whom were mythic Argonauts. Unsurprisingly, many of the expected events in this speech's mythic catalog were won by the expected heroes: running won by Castor, boxing won by Polydeuces, pancratium won by Heracles, wrestling won by Peleus, as well as other events won by other heroic champions. Significantly, however, this oration also alludes to a boat race at Isthmia, won by the magical *Argo* itself, and a music contest where Orpheus won with his lyre.[60] While there is only the thinnest evidence that the Isthmian Games featured boat races, there was clearly much more to the Isthmian festival than merely copying the athletic program of Olympia. The literary accounts suggest a scene of raucous activity and continuous excitement.

In a different oration (the eighth), Dio Chrysostom describes the crowd that assembled for the Isthmian Games. In his comments about the career of the fourth-century-BCE Cynic philosopher Diogenes of Sinope, Dio Chrysostom paints a vivid portrait of the city of Corinth and its character as a crossroads of the ancient world. His account of Diogenes's visit to Isthmia suggests a terrifically cacophonous din, quite different from the reverence and awe that are customary in contemporary places of worship and the relative quiet of the mostly deserted modern-day archaeological site. Dio notes an assemblage of oral performers, indicating that it was customary for "crowds of wretched sophists" to gather around the Temple of Poseidon, arguing with one another, while writers read aloud from their compositions, poets recited their poems to occasional applause, and jugglers, fortune-tellers, lawyers, and peddlers offered their services and advertised their wares. It is into this uproar that Dio Chrysostom casts his retelling of the philosopher Diogenes's visit to the Isthmian Games and the Cynic's condemnation of the frivolity of athletic competition in the face of the true achievements of overcoming the hardships of life.[61]

Similarly, Dio Chrysostom's ninth oration also tells of the philosopher Diogenes's visit to the games at Isthmia. Again, Dio paints a vivid scene of a vibrant festival at Isthmia, with visitors from all over the Greek world, including Asia Minor, Italy, North Africa, Sicily, and the Black Sea region. Dio also describes a splendid scene in which a victor in the one-stade race is carried off by a crowd while fans and onlookers shower him with applause and garlands and ribbons. Although Dio's entertaining tale indicates that Diogenes was critical of the athletes and their accomplishments, the conversation between the philosopher and the victorious runner neatly encapsulates the glory of victory at Isthmia in particular and the Crown Games in general. As Diogenes points out to the runner that his victory has come by only a single stride, the athlete agrees, telling the grumpy philosopher that "this is what made the victory so wondrous."[62] Although Dio Chyrostom's retelling is surely fictionalized and dramatized, it nevertheless offers a compelling portrait of the exciting festival atmosphere at the Isthmian Games.

Dio Chrysostom's depiction suggests a turbulent and tumultuous crowd in the sanctuary of Poseidon as philosophers, sophists, orators, and poets tried to outdo and outperform one another. In this context, Broneer suggested, the early Christian apostle Paul was drawn to Corinth, and specifically to the Isthmian Games, to reach a wide cosmopolitan audience in his missionary endeavors.[63] Besides the public spectacle described by Dio Chrysostom, another source offers a more private, secretive glimpse into the Isthmian Games during the Roman imperial period. The 1959 excavation of a well situated about half of a kilometer from the sanctuary of Poseidon revealed a curse tablet, written in Greek letterforms that date from Roman imperial times. A robust corpus of curse tablets connected to athletics comes from many areas in the ancient Greco-Roman world. This particular tablet from Isthmia depicts and names four individuals and adjures some unnamed but undoubtedly spooky entity to ensure that these men "not prevail in running," presumably in the Isthmian Games. The tablet then includes a considerable amount of typical magical designs and words, intended to invoke supernatural forces that would fulfill the curse. David R. Jordan's interpretation of this curse connected some of its terminology and the diagrams to places elsewhere in the Mediterranean, underscoring again the cosmopolitan nature of the Isthmian Games.[64]

The Roman Period

During the Roman period, the sanctuary and facilities at Isthmia experienced considerable development. In addition to the theater and bath structures, an inscription at Corinth from the latter part of the second century CE describes the contributions at Isthmia of a Roman benefactor named Publius Licinius Priscus Juventianus. According to the inscription, Priscus paid for the remodeling of a stoa near the stadium at Isthmia to include fifty rooms for competing athletes. The inscription also lists several altars, shrines, and dedications in the sanctuary, including the Palaimonion, that benefited from Priscus's generosity.[65] Many of these altars and embellishments have not yet been identified at Isthmia, reminding us of how meagerly the surviving monuments reflect the complexity and variety of the site's history. A brief comment in Plutarch underscores just how little we know about the competitions at ancient Isthmia. Astonishingly, he mentions a golden tablet at Delphi dedicated by a woman named Aristomache who had won twice at Isthmia in the contest of epic poetry.[66] With no additional context, details, or surviving evidence, we are left to wonder about the possibility of female competitors at Isthmia and other Crown Games sites, a tantalizing avenue of inquiry (to be investigated more thoroughly in chapter 6).

For now, however, the questions on these subjects outnumber the answers, and I am limited to observing simply that, well into the Common Era, the Isthmian Games enjoyed widespread acclaim and popularity. Now that we have visited three of the four sites of the Crown Games in the order in which they were held, it is time to turn to the most dramatic geographic location in our *periodos*. With victories at Olympia, Nemea, and Isthmia, the remaining goal for an elite ancient Greek athlete was to win a crown of laurel in the Pythian Games at Delphi.

CHAPTER 5

Delphi and the Pythian Games

All of Mount Parnassus is considered sacred.

—Strabo 9.3.1

All the artists . . . hymn your glory, god, famed for playing the kithara, son of great Zeus, beside this snow crowned peak, O you who reveal to all mortals the eternal and infallible oracles.

—Hymn to Apollo inscribed on the wall of the Athenian Treasury at Delphi, trans. Thomas Mathiesen

Perched high on the slopes of Mount Parnassus, the site of ancient Delphi awes its visitors with its dramatic setting. Five hundred fifty meters above sea level, overlooking a steep mountain valley,[1] this spot was considered to be the center of the world by the ancient Greeks. According to myth, Zeus once simultaneously released two eagles at the edges of the world and sent them flying, one heading east and the other west, until they met at Delphi, in the middle of the world.[2] Although the Pythian Games were second only to the Olympian festival in prestige, the extensive remains of the sanctuary of Apollo and its renowned oracle have (justifiably) dominated both ancient and modern discussions of the site. The Roman-era writer Strabo noted that, although it had been neglected during his time, around the first century CE, the sanctuary had been greatly esteemed throughout history, as shown by

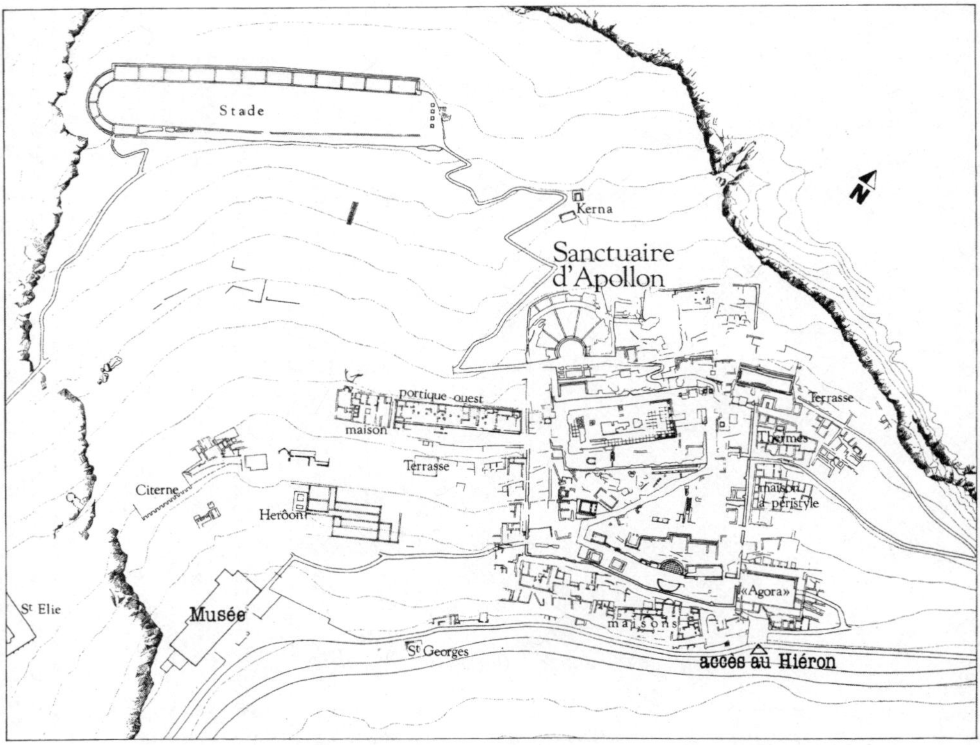

Site plan of the sanctuary of Apollo in ancient Delphi. Drawing by Didier Laroche, 1988, École français d'Athènes. Image courtesy of the École française d'Athènes.

the treasuries, the lavish dedications, the works of the best artists, the number of oracles, and the Pythian Games.[3] As at Olympia, the cult sanctuary and oracle long predated athletic competition at Delphi. Unlike for the Olympian Games, however, the foundation myth for the Pythian Games featured the achievement of an Olympian god, Apollo.

The Foundation Myth

According to tradition, the first Panhellenic version of the Pythian Games at Delphi took place in 582 BCE.[4] These games, sacred to Apollo, have a different type of mythic foundation story than the other Crown Games. Leaving aside a single late reference to Zeus founding the Olympian Games, the Olympian, Isthmian, and Nemean festivals were founded to honor heroic figures. However, the *Homeric Hymn to Apollo* tells a different kind of story.

The *Homeric Hymns* are so-called because many ancient Greeks attributed them to the great epic poet Homer, and their metrical schemes are similar to the Homeric epics the *Iliad* and the *Odyssey*. Although textual and literary criticism disproved the possibility of Homer's authorship even in antiquity, the *Hymns* are a valuable source for early Greek myth. Generally believed to be one of the oldest of the *Hymns*, the *Hymn to Apollo* traces the story of the immortal son of Zeus and Leto and how he came to establish his sanctuary and oracle at Delphi. The ancient composer of this hymn tried to explain the etiology, or origin, of the sanctuary using word similarities. Although the linguistic connections are a bit forced, the hymn nevertheless lays out the basic myth about how the sanctuary of Apollo came to be established at Delphi.

The hymn relates that, as the god Apollo wandered through the Greek world, he came to a pleasing spot in a region of central Greece called Boeotia, near the site of Thebes. However, as he began to devise a plan for establishing a temple on the spot, the nymph Telphusa, who lived there, dissuaded Apollo from settling there permanently. She told him of a better spot to the west, near Mount Parnassus, where his temple would receive more devotion and attention from mortals. Accordingly, Apollo traveled to Parnassus and announced his intention to build a temple and establish an oracle on the spot.

This site on Mount Parnassus, however, was a dangerous one. A terrible dragon (or snake—the word for both in ancient Greek is *drakon*) lived near the site, at the Castalian Spring just a small distance away from Apollo's intended sanctuary. This monster terrorized the inhabitants of the region, and the duplicitous Telphusa had sent Apollo into a trap. Unafraid, "far-shooting Apollo" killed the monster with an arrow from his bow.[5] As it writhed in pain, Apollo taunted the beast to "rot now, here on the earth," and he watched it die.[6] The ancient Greek word for "rot" is similar to the word "python," and the composer of the *Hymn to Apollo* connected Apollo's taunting of the beast "to rot" to the death of the python and the foundation of the Pythian Games. After killing the beast, Apollo set up his sanctuary and oracle at Delphi and punished Telphusa for good measure.[7]

All of the ancient sources for this myth agree that there had long been an oracle at Delphi. Some declare that the oracle was administered by the goddess Earth (Ge). Others indicated that Ge delegated the oracle power to her offspring, the dragon (Python). A Roman-era source, Hyginus, suggests that Apollo took over the oracular duties and then established funeral games in Python's honor, games that became the Pythian Games.[8] As is typical of ancient Greek myth, the story presents some problematic questions and contradictions such as: Why institute games to honor a bloodthirsty monster? Nevertheless, Delphi and the Pythian Games were closely connected to Apollo and the oracle at Delphi.

The Excavations at Delphi

Until the nineteenth century, the ancient site of Delphi featured a small village built atop the sanctuary. The presence of Kastri, described by a Danish archaeologist in 1811 as a "wretched little village," impeded early attempts to investigate the archaeology of the sanctuary.[9] German visitors to the site in the 1830s and 1840s managed to identify some of the foundation walls of the ancient structures, but the scattered collection of the village houses made systematic digging impossible. In 1880, a French archaeologist uncovered the Stoa of the Athenians along the ancient Sacred Way, but it took ten more years before the Greek and French governments were able to conclude an agreement for the excavations to proceed.[10]

In 1891, the French government set aside 500,000 francs for the excavation at Delphi, and the government of Greece supported the effort. Around three hundred property owners had to be bought out and a new village constructed for them a mile or so down the road. The removal of the villagers of Kastri was not altogether a smooth process: when excavations on the site finally began in October 1892, a group of the dispossessed villagers set on the workers and disrupted the recently laid railway, and control of the site was regained only after a "*haute lutte*" (high struggle) and the intervention of the Greek army.[11]

Although many of the site's architectural features were identified and excavated within a couple of decades, work at Delphi is ongoing, with periodic revisions and reinterpretations of the great endeavor. The results of the excavations at Delphi were published seasonally in the *Bulletin de correspondance hellénique* (*BCH*) by the École française d'Athènes, with comprehensive findings and conclusions (and revised conclusions) published in the Fouilles de Delphes series.

The Sanctuary of Athena Pronoia

Set high in the mountains, Delphi enjoyed a commanding view to the south, and ancient pilgrims dutifully climbed the heights of Parnassus to visit the site. In the words of Pausanias, the ascent to Delphi was "difficult even for an active man."[12] The extreme slopes of the mountainside caused the dedicatory offerings and buildings to crowd together, and the athletic facilities associated with the Pythian Games were spread out along the mountainside. As visitors arrived at Delphi and came to the lower part of the sanctuary, they encountered the sanctuary of Athena. Even in ancient times, it was unclear whether the name of this particular temple referred to Athena Pronoia (foresight) or Athena Pronaia (in front of the temple—i.e., the Temple of Athena in front of the Temple of Apollo). A variety of altars, treasuries, and dedications dotted this part of the sanctuary, including the round tholos structure so often featured in tourist photographs of Delphi. The Athena sanctuary was dramatically enlarged during the second half of the sixth century BCE, and excavations there have revealed the remains of an elaborate athletic facility.

Pausanias records that the gymnasium at Delphi was situated between the sanctuary of Athena Pronoia and the Castalian Spring.[13] Sure enough, excavators readily located the site beneath a small monastery, right where Pausanias indicates.[14] Other than Pausanias's brief mention, the written evidence of this gymnasium at Delphi is sparse, with the earliest mention of the site occurring in two heavily restored inscriptions attributed to the fourth century BCE.[15] Flat space was rare in this ruggedly mountainous region, and it appears that this sole gymnasium was employed by the citizens of Delphi as well as those preparing for Panhellenic competitions every four years. As in other cities, the gymnasium was more than just a facility for exercise. As was typical for Greek gymnasiums during the Hellenistic and Roman periods, the complex served as an important civic center, and the (male) citizens of Delphi convened in the gymnasium for education and instruction. Indeed, Jean Jannoray notes that recovered inscriptions from Delphi's gymnasium dating to the Hellenistic and Roman periods honor patrons as diverse as a grammarian, a rhetorician, and an astronomer.[16]

The gymnasium at Delphi featured a palaestra, a pool conveniently filled by the nearby Castalian Spring, and a running track (*xystus*), part of it covered and part of it in open air. Excavators have dated the construction of the gymnasium, palaestra, and *xystus* to around 330 BCE, and it was regularly maintained and updated into the Roman era.[17] Epigraphic and literary evidence indicates that, in addition to the athletic facilities located below the Castalian Spring, this area also featured a sanctuary of Demeter (linked, perhaps, with the worship of Ge, or Earth), as well as hero shrines dedicated to the otherwise unknown heroes Phylakos and Autonoös.[18]

In 1896, excavators at Delphi discovered a damaged Hellenistic-period inscription that describes the expenses associated with preparing the gymnasium and the sanctuary for the Pythian festival.[19] The fastidious accounting in this inscription offers considerable detail about the nature and preparation of the athletic facilities at Delphi. The majority of efforts were focused on preparing the athletic surfaces, and the inscription allots funds for the gymnasium, the covered track (*xystus*), stadium, and hippodrome at Delphi. The gymnasium complex in the lower sanctuary at Delphi is especially significant because it represents one of the earliest preserved examples from the ancient Greek world (dating to the later 300s BCE) and because it conforms largely to the Roman architect-writer Vitruvius's description of an ideal palaestra, featuring covered porticos, an exposed courtyard, and a covered track to protect exercising athletes from the elements.[20]

Leaving the lower portion of the sanctuary, the path to the main sanctuary climbs past the Castalian Spring and arrives at the large sanctuary of Apollo. In describing the site, Pausanias comments on the steepness of the slope, and any visitor would agree with his assessment that the site is huge and steep and a complex jumble of buildings, dedications, and offerings.[21]

The Sanctuary of Apollo

Archaeological excavations have revealed a Bronze Age presence at Delphi, and the oracle was certainly functioning by the end of the Iron Age. Like Olympia, this site featured religious rituals and votive dedications long before the introduction of the Panhellenic athletic festival. Unlike the other Panhellenic sanctuaries, from at least the early sixth century BCE, the sanctuary of Apollo at Delphi was managed by a council of representatives from the surrounding regions and cities, a group called the Delphic Amphictyony.[22] Under the management of this council, the sanctuary underwent extensive expansion and renovations during the first half of the sixth century BCE, and the Pythian festival was expanded at this time to become one of the Panhellenic Crown Games.

The Sacred Way and the Treasuries

After the Temple of Apollo burned down in the middle of the sixth century BCE, the Amphictyonic Council expanded and embellished the sanctuary of Apollo, allowing participating city-states to erect new and remodeled dedications on the site. The Sacred Way, winding its way up the hillside toward the Temple of Apollo, the theater, and the stadium on top, eventually became crowded with dedicatory treasuries, votive statues, and thank offerings—many of them connected to victory in war and victory in athletics. Even Pausanias seems to have been somewhat daunted by the sheer number of monuments along the road, indicating that he would record only the dedications that seemed "most memorable," eschewing the records of athletes and "obscure musicians."[23] The Sacred Way was a place for the Greek city-states to vie with one another for reputation and status. The initial stretch of the Sacred Way featured a Spartan monument proclaiming Sparta to be the "acropolis of Greece" while the other side of the path held a monument erected to commemorate an Arcadian victory over Sparta.[24] Pilgrims approaching the Temple of Apollo along the Sacred Way would have happened upon dozens of these dedications, including the famous Sphinx of Naxos (ca. 575 BCE), spoils from the dramatic Athenian victory over the Persians at Marathon in 490 BCE, and the tripod commemorating the unified Greek victory over the Persians in 479 BCE.

Archaic-period residents on the small Aegean island of Siphnus took advantage of their rich gold and silver mines to build an elaborate treasury prominently situated along the Sacred Way.[25] The sculpted frieze of the treasury featured the Gigantomachy (a mythic battle between the gods and giants) as well as a scene in which Apollo and Heracles wrestle for the god's oracular tripod. According to Apollodorus, when the Pythia refused to grant an oracular pronouncement to Heracles, the hero seized the tripod and carried it away, intending to set up his own oracular seat (that, presumably, would provide oracles whenever he wanted). The god Apollo, seeing his sanctuary under attack, intervened, and the two grappled for the oracular tripod, a scene often portrayed in Greek art toward the end of the Archaic period and one consistent with the competitive context of ancient Greece in general and the Crown Games in particular.[26]

Farther along the Sacred Way, the Athenian Treasury and colonnade occupied a prominent spot near the switchback bend in the pathway. Although there was a smaller structure on the site in the sixth century BCE, Pausanias indicates that the Athenians constructed the building with the spoils from their victory in the Battle of Marathon in 490 BCE.[27] From 1893 to 1894, archaeologists excavated this building and managed to reerect its surviving pieces. This building is the first to have brought together the stories of Theseus and Heracles in its metope decorations, and both of these heroes are depicted in athletic poses as they undertake and accomplish their sundry labors.[28]

The walls of the Treasury of the Athenians featured a considerable number of inscriptions dating from the Roman period. Along with the names of various Pythian victors, these inscriptions described Athenian participation in the Pythian festival. The late dates for these inscriptions—the mid to late second century BCE—make it difficult to draw any firm conclusions from them about the Athenian presence at Delphi during the Archaic or Classical period. Nevertheless, they offer a compelling picture of what the official Athenian embassy looked like during the Roman period and perhaps a clue about how earlier Athenians celebrated the Pythian festival or other important events at Delphi. The inscriptions indicate that the Athenians sent delegations with hundreds of participants, including priests and priestesses, soldiers and cavalry, a flute player, and a *pyrphoros*, or fire bearer, who renewed the city's sacred fire with fire from Delphi.[29]

In addition to describing the processions from Athens, the second-century-BCE inscriptions on the walls of the Athenian Treasury also featured fragments of three hymns to Apollo, complete with musical notations.[30] The words of the hymns retell the arrival of Apollo at Delphi, his fight against Python, and the institution of the oracle, while of course mentioning the presence of Athenian pilgrims at the sanctuary as well.[31]

The Temple of Apollo

The mythic origins connected with Delphi are evident in the history of the Temple of Apollo. According to Pausanias, the original temple was made of laurel wood, the second temple was built by bees from beeswax and feathers, and the third temple was made of bronze.[32] Whatever its mythic origins, when the Temple of Apollo burned down in 548 BCE, the Amphictyony oversaw its reconstruction in conjunction with an ambitious program of expansion for the sanctuary. A prominent Athenian family called the Alcmaeonids funded a large portion of this rebuilding project, and they paid for a marble facade at their own expense.[33] In the early fourth century BCE, probably after an earthquake, the Temple of Apollo was destroyed yet again, and its rebuilding took several decades. It was the remnants of this fourth-century-BCE temple that archaeologists uncovered during the excavation of the sanctuary. Drawing from archaeology and written descriptions, we know the exterior of this temple was decorated with sculptures of Leto, Artemis, and Apollo, probably on the east side, and the god Dionysus on the west.[34] In the pronaos, famous teachings of the Seven Sages were inscribed on the walls, including "Know thyself" and "Nothing in excess."[35]

The Oracle of Apollo

Strabo succinctly declared the importance of the oracle of Apollo at Delphi by noting its reputation of being "the most truthful" as well as its position as the center of the world.[36] Located underground in the *adyton* within the Temple of Apollo, the oracle offered some of the most famous pronouncements from the ancient Greek world. Despite its fame, the details of the oracle's workings are surprisingly sparse. Consultations were held only on certain days, and long lines of inquirers could form. The priestess, called the Pythia, was a female over fifty years of age. On an oracle day, once purified, the Pythia entered a subterranean room in the Temple of Apollo and sat atop a high tripod, where she awaited the influence of the god, attributed by ancient sources to emissions from the earth. After a series of purificatory and sacrificial rites, the inquirer was led by a priest into the temple, and the priest relayed to the Pythia the inquirer's question. The Pythia's incoherent response was interpreted by the priest, typically into hexameter verse.

The earliest record of an oracle at Delphi comes from Homer, where Agamemnon is credited with consulting Apollo before embarking on the Trojan War.[37] Although the example is mythic, this episode offers compelling evidence for the oracle's early date. The *Homeric Hymn to Apollo*, the plays of Aeschylus and Euripides, and the works of numerous sophists, writers, and historians feature the oracle of Apollo as a key means of communication between the gods and humans. Colonists consulted the oracle before heading out to settle new lands, and military leaders sought its advice for upcoming campaigns. It was an oracle from Delphi that persuaded Leonidas to fight to the death with his three hundred Spartiates at Thermopylae.[38] It was an oracle that promised the Athenians that they would be protected by a "wooden wall" during the conflict with the Persians in 480 BCE, an oracle that was interpreted as anticipating the Greek triumph in the naval battle at Salamis.[39] According to Plutarch, Alexander the Great's visit to the oracle occurred on a day when the Pythia was not permitted to deliver answers. Undeterred, Alexander began to drag the priestess to the temple to compel an oracle, and she declared, "You are invincible, my son!"[40] This was oracle enough for the Macedonian king. It was the oracle at Delphi that told an inquiring Athenian that there was nobody wiser than Socrates the philosopher.[41] Romans, too, consulted the oracle. Apollo's oracle offered advice to the Romans besieging Veii in 396 BCE, and perhaps the oracle's most famous reply was given to Cicero when he asked how to attain the highest fame. To this Roman statesman, the oracle recommended that he make his own nature, not public opinion, the guide to his life.[42] The last recorded oracle, possibly spurious, comes from the reign of the Roman emperor Julian the Apostate in the fourth century CE. According to the story, this oracle informed the emperor that with the triumph of Christianity, Apollo's house had fallen, the fountains were silent, and the god's voice was stilled.[43]

Musical Contests and the Theater at Delphi

It is unknown when the musical competitions began at Delphi, but tradition held that they predated the organization of the Panhellenic Pythian Games in the 580s BCE. Originally, the ancient sources indicate, the only contest at Delphi was the singing of a hymn to Apollo while playing the kithara. Chrysothemis of Crete is credited with the first victory in this hymn competition, and he was supposedly the son of one of the original Cretans brought to the sanctuary by Apollo himself when he established it. The names of other victors follow in Pausanias's account, some of them mythic, as well as the names of many performers seemingly more remarkable for not competing at Delphi. The mythic musician Orpheus, for example, refused to stoop to competing, while Homer and Hesiod lacked the requisite musical skills to accompany their poetic prowess.[44] As this was the original contest held at Delphi, the name of its winner was used as a chronological marker in dating Pythiads, much as the winner of the stade race at Olympia lent his name to the Olympiad.[45] In the 580s BCE, as the Pythian Games became part of the Crown Games circuit, the Amphictyonic Council of Delphi embellished the earlier competitive program and added contests for performances with the aulos, a type of woodwind.

The word "aulos" basically means a tube, and the aulos was closer to the modern clarinet or oboe than to a flute since it required a reed to be played. Indeed, M. L. West castigates the "deplorable habit" of referring to the aulos in English as a flute.[46] The aulos instruments seem to have required a double reed, and the main pipe could be constructed of bone, reed, ivory, wood, or metal. The traditional aulos had five finger holes—four on top and one underneath for the thumb. Artistic representations of the *auletes* (aulos player) with bulging cheeks suggest that playing the instrument required effort, and it was this instrument that Athena threw away in disgust after she caught a glimpse in a mirror of how playing distorted her face. The fifth-century-BCE Athenian Alcibiades did the same.[47] The aulos could be played as a single pipe or as a double pipe: presumably the double pipe played the same tune and added volume and richness to the performance. For the Pythian Games, competing musicians were required to use a specific type and size of aulos instrument, called the Pythikos. The first to win the competition in aulos playing was a musician from Argos named Sakadas, who won the first three times the event was contested.[48]

Pausanias records that the eighth Pythian festival (counting inclusively—that is, twenty-eight years after the introduction of the Panhellenic contests at Delphi, so in 558 BCE or 554 BCE) began to offer competitions in playing the kithara without singing, with Agelaus of Tegea winning the crown.[49] Unlike modern harps, where the strings are of varying lengths, Greek stringed instruments featured strings of the same length. The kithara could be played by strumming or plucking, sometimes with the use of a plectrum (i.e., a pick). One late source indicates that, as with the aulos, the Pythian Games required competing musicians to play a standard kithara called the Pythikon.[50] In addition to requiring standard instruments, the musical contests in the Pythian Games required the competitors to play a certain melody called the Pythian *Nomos*. The word *nomos*, a term that refers to custom and law, suggests set rules about meter and sections, as well as a conservative approach to the performances.[51] With standard instruments and melodies, these musical competitions seem to have valued technique and skill over innovation and creativity. Indeed, musical performances in the ancient Greek world in general seem to have been resistant to change. Pausanias relates that the Spartans once objected to one musician's addition of four strings to his kithara.[52] In Plato's *Republic*, Socrates warns against innovations in music and gymnastics since they threaten society's orderly arrangement.[53]

The Pythian *Nomos* included five sections, and this arrangement was meant to commemorate and celebrate the contest between Apollo and Python. The *Nomos* included sections for prelude, the contest itself, and then praise and celebration for the victorious god.[54] Eventually, the organizers of the Pythian Games introduced other musical contests such as choral competitions and the poetry performances.[55] Other contests were discontinued. For example, Pausanias indicates that the competition in singing to the aulos ended because the tunes were extremely sad.[56] These musical events marked the focal point of the festival, and the games were "centered around musical competitions," as one modern scholar puts it. [57] Later, accomplished guilds of professional artists came to dominate the performances and competitions.

The logistics of the competitive musical events remain elusive to modern scholars. Unlike the gymnastic or equestrian competitions, the musical competitions must have required a certain amount of subjective judgment. The best understanding we have of how musical competitions transpired comes from a very late source. In 1926, archaeologists in Karanis, Egypt, recovered four pieces of papyrus from the first or second century CE with details about rules for musical contests. The provenance of the rules is unknown, as is the festival to which these rules applied. Although quite fragmentary, the rules indicate that performing the Pythian *Nomos* was one of this (presumably Egyptian) festival's contests. The rules declare that performers who omit a portion of the melody are to be disqualified and indicate that the performers' entrances and exits to the performance area were integral parts of the competition as well.[58]

The musical contests of the Pythian Games, as well as the other musical festivals held at Delphi, were conducted in the theater that sat adjacent to the Temple of Apollo, prominently situated on the hillside of the sanctuary. As of 2021, the full results of the excavation of the theater had not been published, and thus much of our knowledge remains incomplete. A recovered inscription indicates that the theater was remodeled in about 160 BCE, and that remodeled theater is the one seen by today's visitors to the sanctuary. It seems likely that the updated theater was built atop an older version, especially considering the topographical limitations posed by the rugged terrain, but this is not certain.[59] In 1895, excavators found fragments of bas-relief sculptures in the theater. Some of these sculptures featured Heracles in the midst of his labors.[60] Others referred to feats accomplished outside of the twelve canonical labors (*athla*), perhaps connected in some way to the Hellenistic-period king Eumenes, a possible benefactor for the theater's renovations. The juxtaposition of the great hero's feats with the site of Delphi's musical competitions would have underscored the heroic connections between the contests of the Crown Games and mythic heroes. Although Heracles was present in the art and imagery at Delphi, it was a different hero, Neoptolemus, the son of Achilles, who enjoyed a hero's shrine close to the temple and theater at Delphi.

Neoptolemus at Delphi

The myths surrounding Neoptolemus (sometimes called Pyrrhus), the son of Achilles, recorded an impressive list of heroic achievements. Most accounts claim that it was Neoptolemus, brought to Troy as a youth after the death of his father, who killed Priam at an altar of Zeus in the courtyard.[61] Eventually, Neoptolemus himself was killed by violence at Delphi. Several convoluted versions disagree on the details. Some accounts claim that Neoptolemus was killed while plundering Apollo's sanctuary, an act of sacrilege Neoptolemus undertook because of the role of Apollo in Achilles's death. Euripides's play *Andromache* has the deranged Orestes kill Neoptolemus for having seized Hermione, Orestes's betrothed.[62] Pausanias adds that Neoptolemus was killed on an altar at Delphi as retribution for his killing Priam at an altar.[63] In still another version, Pindar relates on two occasions that the hero went to Delphi to offer spoils from Troy to Apollo and was killed after a dispute over the sacrificial meat.[64] Despite the confusing details of these contradictory accounts, they all agree that Neoptolemus was killed at Delphi and his tomb was located near the Temple of Apollo.

Pausanias situates the tomb of Neoptolemus to the left as one exited the Temple of Apollo at Delphi, and he mentions another spot close by where he says the hero was killed.[65] Pausanias describes in detail an elaborate painting by Polygnotus nearby, which was intended to be placed above Neoptolemus's tomb. In the painting, Neoptolemus was the only Greek hero depicted as still killing Trojans.[66] Although Pausanias claims a third-century-BCE date for the institution of a cult for Neoptolemus at Delphi, Pindar's *Nemean* 7, written during the fifth century BCE, strongly supports an earlier date, informing the reader (or listener) that Neoptolemus acts as "overseer" of the processions at Delphi for the heroes and their many sacrifices.[67] If we follow this account, it seems that in Pindar's day—that is, the early fifth century BCE—the people of Delphi not only honored Achilles's son with a heroic cult but in fact assigned him a status superior to the other heroes honored at Delphi. In addition, fragmentary references from the roughly contemporary mythographer Pherecydes also support an early date for Neoptolemus's importance at Delphi, although no mention of cult has survived.[68] These earlier writings by Pindar and Pherecydes argue more convincingly for a tomb and cult of Neoptolemus at Delphi in the late Archaic period.

Archaeological excavations in the early twentieth century identified a likely location for a shrine to Neoptolemus. From 1934 to 1935, French archaeologists excavated a rectangular building that measured approximately twelve by eight meters. Preliminary soundings in a portion of the construction revealed evidence of Mycenaean use of the site during the Bronze Age, but it seems unlikely that the site was in continuous use from the Bronze Age into the Classical era. The Mycenaean remains included a wall and a large ceramic storage container, called a pithos, that measured one meter, thirty centimeters in height. Inside this pithos were discovered ashes that contained the charred remains of another vessel. Other findings included statue fragments from the late fifth or early fourth century BCE.[69] While it has been suggested that the burnt remains inside the Mycenaean period pithos might represent a Classical-period continuation or revival of a Bronze Age cult, with the contents of the pithos eventually coming to represent the cremated remains of the hero Neoptolemus, the evidence is too sparse to offer this as anything more than fanciful speculation.[70] A great earthquake and landslide in 1935 wiped out a substantial portion of the excavations, and most of the questions about a cult of Neoptolemus at Delphi continue unanswered.[71]

Thus, the case for assigning this structure to the cult of Neoptolemus must remain circumstantial. This site corresponds with the description offered by Pausanias, and the nature of the surrounding monuments could suggest connections to the son of Achilles. The Daochos statue group, situated directly north of this structure, was dedicated by a prominent family of Thessaly whose holdings were purported to include the ancestral lands of Achilles. The Attalid rulers of Pergamum, who also dedicated their offerings in this area, likewise claimed a connection with Neoptolemus: according to tradition Pergamos, the eponymous hero of Pergamum, was the son of Neoptolemus.[72] Did the Daochos family and the Attalids choose this area for their dedications based on the proximity to the shrine of Neoptolemus? It is certainly possible, but further archaeological investigations are necessary before the four-sided structure to the northeast of Apollo's temple at Delphi can be considered unquestionably the site where the ancient Greeks provided offerings to Neoptolemus.

Despite the uncertainty surrounding the location of a shrine and the conflicting versions of the myth of Neoptolemus at Delphi, the literary references support the existence of a cult in the late fifth or early fourth century BCE. Whether or not the location of Neoptolemus's tomb during the later Archaic period (or earlier) corresponds to the site identified by modern archaeologists, Pindar relates that Neoptolemus "remains next to the well-walled house of the god" at Delphi, implying that the hero's tomb was indeed situated close to the Temple of Apollo.[73] This corresponds to the layout of the other three Crown Games sites, where a hero tomb was featured in close proximity to the main temple and the earliest competition grounds, although fittingly at Delphi, instead of a stadium, the hero's tomb sat next to the theater. Although the topography of Mount Parnassus might have necessitated the construction of the stadium farther up the mountain, the placement of the theater close to the hero's tomb and the Temple of Apollo is appropriate for Delphi, since the musical contests held such a prominent role in the Pythian Games.

The Stadium at Delphi

The steep terrain of Delphi presents a unique difficulty in the four Crown Games sites as there is a shortage of suitable flat space for a stadium or a hippodrome. The stadium at Delphi, perched high above the Temple of Apollo and the theater, at "the highest point of the city,"[74] was a relatively late addition to the sanctuary. Before the construction of this

The Stadium at Delphi. Author's photograph.

stadium, the nonmusical gymnastic and equestrian competitions of the Pythian Games presumably took place somewhere else, with the most likely spot being somewhere far below on the flat land near the sea at a site called Kirrha. Indeed, in *Pythian* 10, Pindar praises a victor for winning a footrace "below the rock of Kirrha," and *Pythian* 11 refers to the "contest at Kirrha," but it is difficult to read these allusions literally.[75] The sites of the earliest stadium and the hippodrome remain undiscovered.

Excavations of the later stadium at Delphi atop the sanctuary of Apollo took place in 1896, with a preliminary plan of the stadium published in 1897.[76] Presumably, the steep mountain setting restricted the size of this stadium, allowing no more than an estimated seven thousand spectators to watch the games there.[77] Nevertheless, what it lacked in size, the stadium at Delphi compensated for in style: Pausanias records that, during the Roman era, Herodes Atticus outfitted the entire stadium with expensive Pentelic marble.[78] The stadium's layout featured a "triumphal arch" at the east end for athletes to enter the track. One excavator commented that the track represented an "extraordinary" feat of engineering, measuring 177.414 meters from one starting line to the other, a mere 6 millimeters away from a length of exactly 600 Roman feet.[79]

Outside the stadium, on the southern wall, a cryptic inscription offers some clues about the date of the stadium's construction, but in some ways the inscription raises more questions than it answers.[80] Translated, the inscription reads: "It is forbidden to carry wine outside of the stadium. If someone carries it out, so that the god for which the mix is made will be appeased, let the malefactor make an offering and pay a penalty of five drachmas, of which half goes to the denouncer."

The ancient Greek word translated here as "outside" is problematic and in dialect.[81] Initially, Théophile Homolle and the other excavators assumed that the inscription forbade taking wine *into* the stadium and offered a reward to those who reported transgressors.[82] In the modern era, this injunction against bringing wine into the stadium has been compared to a crowd-control measure for unruly spectators.[83] Later philological studies, however, have demonstrated that the inscription's key preposition prohibits taking wine *out of*, rather than *into*, the stadium. So the inscription forbids celebrants at some festival (there are a few possibilities, but they probably incorporated the worship of Dionysus) from carrying wine away from the site.

The dialect and letterforms of this inscription are difficult to decipher definitively since the inscription's orthography, dialect, and letterforms seem to date from more than one time period. Homolle dated the inscription to the middle of the fifth century BCE and argued that this indicated the time of the stadium's construction, giving a date of about 448 BCE.[84] However, later reinterpretations significantly altered these conclusions.

In the 1970s, Pierre Aupert reexcavated the stadium, which had sustained heavy damage from erosion and water runoff, and the results were published in 1979.[85] Aupert found practically no evidence for the stadium's existence before the late 300s or even the early 200s BCE, at least 125 years later than Homolle's proposed date for the stadium's construction. Aupert's argument rests on dating of pottery sherds uncovered within the stadium's area. In addition, precise measurements of the stadium's earliest surface revealed some curious features of the starting lines on the western end. For some reason, the starting blocks were installed *on top* of the leveled and prepared surface, requiring the builders to apply an additional layer of dirt to even out the running surface. Besides this curiosity, the starting-line grooves in the stones are unevenly cut. There is a single set of grooves, but they are wider in some of the stones, suggesting that some of these stones were repurposed from another location and "remodeled" to fit together into a unified starting line.[86] In addition to his conclusions about these blocks, Aupert concluded that the large block of stone on the stadium's outside that features the wine inscription showed evidence of having been moved from an earlier location and perhaps updated, accounting for the third-century-BCE orthography in a few places. The evidence therefore suggests that the stadium at Delphi was not built until the end of the fourth or the early third century BCE and that the gymnastic competitions of the Archaic- and Classical-period Pythian Games took place at an as-yet-undetermined site on the coastal plain below Delphi. When the stadium was built high above the Temple of Apollo, some of the features of the earlier stadium were moved to the current site. Perhaps future archaeological investigations will unearth this earlier stadium site.

The four Crown Games sites—Olympia, Nemea, Isthmia, and Delphi—featured important religious centers, the highest pinnacle of athletic competition and achievement, musical competitions, oracles, curses, and an unending stream of athletes and pilgrims eager to honor the gods, participate in the games, or watch the pursuit of athletic immortality and undying. With a greater and stronger appreciation of these four sites in mind, I turn now to the athletes themselves, with an examination of the careers and achievements of the greatest of the Crown Games champions.

CHAPTER 6

Crowned Champions

The Greatest of the Crown Games Athletes

Go into the stadium and become such men
as are worthy of victory.

—PHILOSTRATUS, *APOLLONIUS OF TYANA* 5.43

Who were the best athletes to win in the Crown Games of ancient Greece? Who were the most famous? If one of the goals of ancient athletic victory was to secure "undying *kleos*," whose *kleos* continues to shine into the present day? This chapter examines the careers of the most famous and successful athletic champions from ancient Greece—and these are not always the same people. Although the epinician odes of Pindar, Bacchylides, and others are important sources for understanding the culture of victory in ancient Greek athletics, the poems themselves reveal frustratingly little about the actual lives of the athletes or the stories of their victories.

Pausanias, visiting the sites of the Crown Games hundreds of years after most of the great athletes had competed, recorded many of the stories he heard or read, presumably gathering his information from the inscribed victory monuments themselves. However, even Pausanias expressed some frustration about his lack of knowledge concerning the stories of notable athletes from ancient Greece. As he wrote, not all of the victors at Olympia had statues; indeed, many distinguished athletes had no way to publicize and commemorate their great accomplishments, and these Pausanias found himself unable to record.[1] Besides Pausanias and other literary sources, epigraphy and archaeology offer additional information concerning the most accomplished athletes of ancient Greece. Despite the limitations of our sources, many stories have survived. These stories of victorious (and other) ancient Greek athletes continue to entertain and inspire readers today, just as they did Pausanias and his contemporaries.

The Heroic Athletes

Perhaps the most accomplished and successful athlete from the ancient world was a wrestler from the Greek-speaking region of southern Italy. Milo of Croton dominated the Panhellenic wrestling world in the late sixth century BCE, and his accomplishments accumulated a patina of legend and myth even in ancient times. Milo won Olympian crowns six times, Pythian crowns six times, Isthmian crowns ten times, and Nemean crowns nine times, making him the ancient Greek world's greatest wrestler over a continuous span of over twenty years. Milo's physical strength was legendary in the Greek world, and the stories of his feats are as entertaining as they are unbelievable. For instance, sources claim that he was able to hold a pomegranate in his hands and prevent anyone from prying it free while also protecting the fruit from being crushed. He could tie a cord around his head and break it by holding his breath and expanding the veins in his head. Milo was reputed to have manually carried his own statue into the Altis at Olympia, and he could stand on an oiled discus without slipping as people tried to push him off.

When his city-state of Croton, in Italy, went to war against a neighboring community called Sybaris, it was Milo who led the soldiers of Croton. Instead of donning the armor of a hoplite soldier, however, Milo led the troops to victory while crowned with his six Olympian wreaths, wearing a lion skin, and carrying a club. Clearly, this outstanding athlete modeled himself after the mighty Heracles, and the ancient historian Diodorus Siculus reports that the people of Croton marveled that Milo had personally been "the cause" of their victory.[2] Milo's actions indicate the strong associations between powerful and accomplished athletes, the heroes of myth, and victory in ancient Greece.[3]

During the fourth century BCE, the historian Xenophon wrote that the great heroes of myth made the Greeks "invincible" against their barbarian enemies. The appearance of a hero during or before battle represented a harbinger of victory.[4] The mythic hero Theseus is supposed to have appeared at the Battle of Marathon in 490 BCE as the outnumbered Athenians surprised and defeated the invading Persian forces. Before the Battle of Salamis in 480 BCE, the Greeks sent a ship to Aegina to fetch the statues of the heroes Aeacus and his sons, the most notable of whom were Peleus and Telamon.[5] As at Marathon, the outnumbered Greek forces subsequently defeated the Persians. The heroes Castor and Polydeuces appeared as stars on either side of Lysander's ship during the Battle of Aegospotami in 405 BCE, a great Spartan victory and the culminating battle of the Peloponnesian War.[6] The great Messenian hero Aristomenes reportedly led the Thebans against Sparta at the Battle of Leuctra in 371 BCE.[7]

The presence of these heroes, and their talismanic power, assured victories for the Greeks they were connected to. Thus, the presence of the great athlete Milo, and his heroic, talismanic power—on display through his crowns and his Heraclean attire—assured the people of Croton a victory in their battle. Milo experienced an unusual death. According to the ancient accounts, he came upon a tree that had been partially split, and he tried to finish the separation. Unable to pull the tree apart, Milo's hands became trapped in the cracked tree trunk, and he was devoured by wolves.

Another accomplished athlete from ancient Greece who won great renown in the Crown Games was Polydamas, a pancratiast from Scotussa in Thessaly. Polydamas won a crown in the Olympian Games in 408 BCE and, like Milo, engaged in a number of adventurous exploits that showcased his strength and prowess. His feats, surely exaggerated, reportedly included pulling the hoof from a struggling bull and stopping a moving chariot by grabbing on to it and digging his heels into the ground. At some point, he journeyed east to the court of the Persian king. In some sort of contest, he fought and defeated three members of the king's elite bodyguard simultaneously.[8] Out of an expressed desire to emulate Heracles, Polydamas journeyed to Mount Olympus in northern Greece and killed a large lion with his bare hands. A surviving portion of Polydamas's fourth-century-BCE statue base at Olympia shows the great athlete fighting a lion, linking this story more closely to the athlete's lifetime.[9] These heroic actions brought Polydamas some type of heroic status among the Greeks, since after his death, his statue was said to heal the sick.[10] Polydamas's athletic and heroic might, as well as his *arete*, afforded his memory a degree of supernatural or superhuman power.

Not all ancient Greeks were fans of Polydamas. At Pellene, a city in

Achaea in the Peloponnese, Pausanias describes a statue of a Pellenean soldier situated in the city's gymnasium. The soldier was Promachus, the son of Dryon, who won the pancratium three times at Isthmia, twice at Nemea, and once at Olympia, defeating the great Polydamas after he returned from Persia. According to a different ancient author, Philostratus, Promachus's trainer spurred the athlete to his Olympian victory with a clever stratagem. The trainer told Promachus that the woman Promachus loved would begin to return his love if he managed to win at Olympia. Inspired, Promachus defeated Polydamas and claimed the Olympian crown. In fact, the trainer had not consulted the woman at all, and Philostratus neglects to tell us how Promachus's love interest reacted to this victory.[11] Although Pausanias saw the statue and the inscription about Promachus in Achaea, the Thessalians in Polydamas's homeland disagreed with this account. They rejected the notion that Polydamas had been beaten and dismissed the claims of the Pelleneans.[12]

Theagenes of Thásos was another fifth-century-BCE heavy-event athlete who achieved heroic status after his death.[13] An accomplished boxer and pancratiast, Theagenes won both of these events at the same Olympian Games around the year 480 BCE. In all, he won at least two crowns at Olympia, three at Delphi, in addition to nine Nemean and ten Isthmian championships. As with Milo and Polydamas, the stories of Theagenes's life have accumulated a good deal of mythic exaggeration. For instance, the epigram that adorned his statue reportedly claimed that he once ate an entire ox (in one sitting), and as a boy he is supposed to have carried a large bronze statue he admired home from his city's marketplace. Like the other athletic would-be heroes, Theagenes is reported to have consciously sought association with his mythic predecessors. Out of "ambitious envy of Achilles," the swiftest of the Greek heroes in the *Iliad*, Theagenes abandoned combat sports for running and won a long-distance race in the Thessalian hometown of Achilles.[14] Other sources assert that the people of Thásos associated their athletic champion with Heracles, claiming that Theagenes was really the son of that immortal hero instead of the mortal man who raised him, although his victory inscriptions listed Timoxenos as his father.

One story goes that after Theagenes's death, one of his enemies regularly went to the athlete's statue on Thásos at night and flogged it out of hatred for the dead man. When one night the statue fell on the enemy and killed him, the dead man's sons prosecuted the statue for murder, and the people of Thásos threw it into the sea. Later, to dispel a crippling famine, the people of Thásos fished up the statue, rededicated it, and offered sacrifices to it as a divinity.[15] Jean Pouilloux, one of the excavators of Theagenes's shrine on Thásos, has suggested that the statue's "trial" took place in the fifth century BCE, between 440 and 420, within a generation or so of Theagenes's athletic victories in the early to mid-fifth century BCE.[16] In addition, Pausanias claims to know of statues of Theagenes in many other locations that possessed the ability to cure diseases.[17] Clearly, Theagenes's impressive exploits as an athlete and a heroic imitator brought his memory divine recognition and heroic status after his death.

In 1939 on the island of Thásos, French archaeologists unearthed a small stone treasury or deposit box for offerings to Theagenes in the foundations of the hero's shrine in the ancient agora, or marketplace.[18] Seventy-three centimeters in height, the cylindrical treasury displayed two inscriptions and has been dated by its stratigraphic location and its epigraphic features to the end of the first century BCE. The earlier of these inscriptions regulated monetary offerings to the heroic athlete. It required those coming to sacrifice to Theagenes to deposit a one-obol offering through the opening in the top of the stone treasury. The second inscription, somewhat fragmentary, much briefer, and inscribed later, probably during the first century CE, promises good fortune to the giver and the giver's family. In addition, in his hero shrine at Thásos, archaeologists uncovered fragments of an inscription that listed the athlete's many Panhellenic victories, and copies of this same inscription have also been found at Delphi and Olympia. The opening lines of the version from Delphi, the most complete survivor of the three, highlights the separation between the mighty Theagenes and ordinary mortals:

> You, son of Timoxenos . . .
> For never at Olympia has the same man been crowned
> for victory in boxing and in pancration.
> But you, of your three victories in the Pythian Games, won one unopposed,
> A feat which no other mortal man has accomplished.
> In nine Isthmian Games, you won ten times. For twice
> the herald proclaimed your victories to the ring of mortal onlookers
> in boxing and pancration on the very same day.
> Nine times, Theogenes, you won at the Nemean Games.

> And you won thirteen hundred victories in the lesser contests.
> Nobody, I declare, defeated you in boxing for twenty-two
> years.[19]

The institution of an elaborate cult in the city center on Thásos for the great athlete within a century of his death, most likely within only two or three generations, demonstrates the significance of Theagenes's victories. His memory remained powerful enough to merit an expanded cult that lasted for hundreds of years in the Hellenistic and Roman periods. His great victories, including his imitation of the hero Achilles, brought him heroic honors on Thásos and in many other places among both Greeks and barbarians.[20]

Another prominent athlete who achieved some measure of immortality was Euthymus of Western Locri, a site in southern Italy. Euthymus was active at the same time as Theagenes, and in 484 BCE, Euthymus won an Olympian crown in boxing. Euthymus and Theagenes were apparently more than just passing rivals. According to Pausanias, in 480 BCE, Theagenes entered the boxing competition at Olympia and managed to defeat Euthymus, the defending champion, although Theagenes was then too spent to win his expected crown in pancratium. Sensing that Theagenes had entered boxing merely to spite Euthymus, the *hellanodikai* fined Theagenes the hefty sum of two talents, one of which went to Euthymus. It appears that Theagenes learned his lesson, paid his fine, and did not enter the boxing competitions at Olympia in future festivals. Euthymus subsequently won the next two boxing crowns at Olympia.[21] While there must be more detail to this story than Pausanias managed to preserve, it is not difficult to imagine that a quarrel between two elite, heavy-hitting athletes such as Theagenes and Euthymus could have produced an extraordinarily violent boxing match in 480 BCE. It seems likely that Theagenes did more injury to Euthymus than merely entering the same competition.

Euthymus's story does not end with his vindication, however. Pausanias also records that, when Euthymus returned to Italy, he came to the village of Temesa, where the people were under the curse of a restless spirit that demanded the sacrifice of a young woman every year. In typically heroic fashion, Euthymus just happened to be passing by when the people were locking the young woman in the temple where the bloodthirsty ghost would appear. Euthymus strapped on his armor, fought the ghost, and drove it out of the land and under the sea, where it never bothered the people of Temesa again. As expected in a story of this type, Euthymus married the rescued girl and eventually transformed into a heroic figure, receiving honors and offerings after his death.[22]

Milo, Polydamas, Theagenes, and Euthymus were exceptional athletes, and the fullness of the accounts of their achievements, as embellished as they may be, is a rare feature of these extraordinary champions. The stories of most athletic victors from ancient Greece are much briefer and focus on a single element of the athlete's notoriety or reputation. The stories also focus overwhelmingly on Olympian victories, often leaving out accounts of athletic excellence at Delphi, Nemea, and Isthmia. Nevertheless, although brief, many of these accounts are richly rewarding to read, both for understanding the culture and norms of ancient Greek athletic culture and for pure entertainment.

Athletic Champions in the Crown Games

In 408 BCE, Eubotas of Cyrene (a city-state in Northern Africa) showed up to the ninety-third Olympian festival with his victory statue already made. Although such hubristic behavior typically would have invited the scorn of mortals and the wrath of the gods, Eubotas avoided any such accusations. He claimed that the oracle at Siwa (a site in modern Egypt) had foretold his Olympian victory, and thus having a ready-made statue represented his dedication to the will of the gods rather than the arrogance of a mortal. And so Eubotas was able to dedicate his statue on the same day he won his victory in the stade race.[23] When a runner named Ageus won the *dolichos* (long-distance) race at Olympia in 328 BCE, he is said to have run home to Argos to announce his triumph personally, a distance of about 160 kilometers (100 miles).[24] Astyanax, a pancratiast from Miletus (a well-known city on the coast of Asia Minor), won Olympian crowns three times in a row. After he returned home to Asia Minor, he was invited to meet and dine with a local Persian governor named Ariobarzanes. At the reception, Astyanax ate all of the food prepared for himself and the eight other guests, and when the great athlete died, two funeral urns were required to contain all of his ashes.[25]

Death in the Crown Games

Although he won two pancratium crowns at Olympia in the 500s BCE, a renowned but unexpected third victory came to Arrhachion (sometimes spelled Arrichion) around 564 BCE. According to Pausanias, although Arrhachion's (unnamed and unremembered) opponent held him tight in a choke hold, Arrhachion managed to dislocate his adversary's toe, causing the opponent to surrender just as Arrhachion died of suffocation. Pausanias noted that Arrhachion's victory came from his *arete*, as well as from the "justice of the judges."[26] Later Greeks routinely commemorated the perseverance, toughness, and achievement of Arrhachion and scorned the last-second surrender of his unnamed homicidal opponent—on account of a sore toe.[27]

Arrhachion earned considerable renown through his posthumous victory, but just how common was death in the ancient Crown Games? Despite several stories in ancient Greek myth concerning death by discus, there is no known historical episode of such an ill-fated throw.[28] At Athens, where most of the best sources for modern knowledge of ancient Greek laws originate, there were several mentions of the legal process for handling "unwilling" or involuntary killing in athletic contexts. Typically, death in an athletic competition was not considered homicide or even manslaughter. However, the sources are clear that the athletic killing must have been done "unwillingly."[29] But the heavy combat sports of boxing and pancratium offered a potential dilemma.

It is worth remembering that these sports in ancient Greece were different from today's versions—there were no timed rounds, scored points, or weight divisions. Boxers and pancratiasts fought until one opponent gave up or was rendered unconscious or—occasionally—died. It is hard to excuse an athlete who killed another in pancratium or boxing as having done so completely "unwillingly," since the basic premise of the competition was to violently kick, punch, or otherwise batter an opponent into submission. However, ancient Greek taboos about bloodguilt posed a quandary for the games' judges. How could the judges reward impressive victory but also condemn intentional killing or manslaughter? From the limited information available, it seems that the judges often chose to disqualify the winner, perhaps on questionable grounds, to avoid rewarding a killer. This plausibly fits the circumstances for Arrhachion's victory, considering the improbability that his opponent surrendered in the championship match of this brutal event because of a painful toe. With the story of Damoxenos and Creugas, it is even more apparent that this is what happened.

Again, I turn to Pausanias for my information. In around 400 BCE, an otherwise unknown Syracusan named Damoxenos killed his opponent, Creugas, while boxing at the Nemean Games. According to the story, the final bout dragged on toward night, and it was necessary to end the match before darkness fell. The two competitors agreed to allow each other a single unopposed blow in an attempt to bring the contest to a speedy conclusion. Creugas struck first, landing a punch to his opponent's head. Then Damoxenos asked Creugas to lift an arm, and he jammed his fingers into Creugas's side between the ribs. With his hand embedded in his opponent's torso, Damoxenos grabbed a handful of entrails and pulled them out, causing poor Creugas to die on the spot. The Argives who were administering the Nemean Games—presumably after they recovered from the shock—disqualified Damoxenos, determining that he had, in fact, landed several blows (one for each finger) instead of the agreed-upon single punch. Accordingly, Creugas was awarded the victory posthumously, and a statue was erected for him at Corinth.[30] As with the story of Arrhachion, the series of events is a little difficult to accept. Setting aside the physiological improbabilities of this story, the fact that Damoxenos's blow killed his competitor placed the Argive judges into the problematic situation of potentially condoning a murder by awarding the victor's crown to a killer. The technical explanation set forth by Pausanias—that Damoxenos had actually landed several blows instead of just one—seems overly legalistic. However, it presents a plausible reason to disqualify the apparent champion and to avoid the social taboo of honoring a killer, a killer who seemed all too "willing" to kill his opponent.

In addition to the story of Damoxenos, Pausanias provides the bulk of information about a boxer named Cleomedes of Astypalaea. In the Olympian Games of 492 BCE, Cleomedes defeated his opponent, Iccus of Epidaurus, by beating him to death. This time, Pausanias relates no details of last-second surrender or a legalistic decision. In this case, the Olympian judges simply disqualified Cleomedes for "committing unjust deeds."[31] We read that Cleomedes, stripped of his victory, lost his mind with grief. He returned to Astypalaea, where he pulled a supporting pillar from a school, causing the roof to collapse and kill sixty boys. Fleeing the angry townspeople, Cleomedes hid inside a chest in the sanctuary of Athena. When his pursuers broke the chest open, Cleomedes had disappeared. An inquiry to the Delphic oracle elicited a response that the people of Astypalaea should worship Cleomedes as "the last of the heroes."[32] Heroization seems a strange reward for a murderous and manic boxer. Perhaps this story preserves an element of the tension that existed at the Crown Games between rewarding an impressive, violent victory and excusing an intentional killing.

The Political Champions

A number of Crown Games champions enjoyed a high degree of political and military success during and after their athletic careers. This is not entirely surprising, since athletics were a favorite pastime of aristocratic elites who possessed the time and resources to train and compete at the highest levels. Other athletes used their victories as springboards into political, military, and civic stations. After all, *kleos* was an important indicator of an athlete's *arete*, and leaders constantly sought to demonstrate their worthiness to rule.

Although he is more famous for his role as a third-century-BCE political and military leader in the Achaean League, Aratus of Sicyon also participated in the Crown Games. Aratus won crowns in the pentathlon, although the source that records this gives no additional details, implying that these victories were won in lesser festivals. Aratus's Olympian victory came in a chariot race, and he erected a statute at Olympia to commemorate his achievement.[33] This is the same Aratus who held alternative Nemean Games in 235 BCE and who ordered the capture and enslavement of those journeying to the other version of the games being held at Argos.[34] Clearly, Aratus understood the political importance of conducting, competing in, and winning in the Crown Games.

Like Aratus, Melissus of Thebes was known for competing both as an athlete and in the role of the owner of a chariot. A fifth-century-BCE athlete, Melissus is remembered in two of Pindar's odes, remarkably for victories in different events. *Isthmian* 3 indicates that Melissus won at Isthmia in a chariot competition, where he presumably owned the winning chariot. In *Isthmian* 4, which commemorates Melissus's victory in pancratium, Pindar praises the athlete as possessing the heart of a lion and the cunning of a fox.[35]

A great athlete named Chaeron of Pellene represents an example of what not to do in a political career after athletic success. The people of Pellene, a city on the northern coast of the Peloponnese, avoided commemorating Chaeron because of his political career that followed his athletic victories. Victorious four times at Olympia and twice at Isthmia in wrestling, he ranked among the greatest athletes of the fourth century BCE. However, he acquired infamy by accepting a position as dictator of his city under the patronage of Alexander the Great. Although he was a pupil of Plato, Chaeron was not an idealized "philosopher king." Instead, he exiled his enemies and confiscated their property while he ruled Pellene. Later Pelleneans "never even mentioned" Chaeron, because of the way he had treated the citizens of his city.[36]

Perhaps the finest athlete produced by the city-state of Athens during the Classical era was Callias, the son of Didymias. Callias was a fifth-century-BCE pancratiast who won multiple victories in the Crown Games. According to an inscription recovered from the Athenian acropolis, Callias won once at Olympia, twice at Delphi, five times at Isthmia, four times at Nemea, and more times than worth remembering at the Panathenaea.[37] Pausanias places Callias and his Olympian victory in the seventy-seventh Olympian festival—that is, in 472 BCE.[38] Like other notable athletic victors, Callias apparently had a respectable political career, as his name appears on some recovered Athenian ostraca.[39]

Pausanias took the rare step of recording verbatim the commemorative inscription from the victory monument of Chilon from Patrae, a settlement in the northern Peloponnese, that dates to the last third of the fourth century BCE (ca. 330 BCE). As Pausanias writes, Chilon won in wrestling twice at Olympia and twice at Delphi, three times at Nemea and four times at Isthmia. Chilon's inscription was written posthumously, though, as it indicates that he died in battle.[40]

Like Callias of Athens, Diagoras won great renown as an Olympian boxer and occupied a prominent position among the political and ruling elites of his home city on the island of Rhodes during the middle of the fifth century BCE. Pindar characterizes Diagoras, the subject of his *Olympian* 7, as a "straight-fighting, mighty man" and alludes to a victory at Delphi.[41]

Diagoras, however, is especially notable for his family of Olympian competitors and victors, a genealogy that spanned three generations. Pausanias indicates that Diagoras and his family enjoyed a group of statues at Olympia among the other statues from Rhodes, and it was indeed a remarkable family.[42] Diagoras won an Olympian crown for boxing as an adult. His three sons also won Olympian events in the combat sports: Acusilaus won in boxing, Damagetus was a pancratium champion, and Dorieus, the youngest, won pancratium three consecutive times. Dorieus also won eight times at Isthmia, seven at Nemea, and once at the Pythian Games by forfeit—that is, no opponents dared challenge him.

Pausanias is clear that Acusilaus and Diagoras won their victories at

Olympia in the men's category. It is unclear how many of Dorieus's and Damagetus's victories were won in the boys' category and how many in the men's. Nevertheless, this impressive family held a dominant position in Olympian competitions that spanned generations. As the story goes, when Acusilaus and Damagetus won their crowns at Olympia, they carried their father, a former champion, on their shoulders as a throng of Greeks threw flowers and shouted congratulations. Plutarch tells us that a Spartan greeted Diagoras by telling him, "Die now, Diagoras. You cannot climb Mount Olympus!"[43] That is, Diagoras had done everything a mortal could hope to do.

Besides his numerous athletic victories, Diagoras's son Dorieus enjoyed widespread fame and infamy in the Greek world. During the Peloponnesian War (431–404 BCE), he fought against Athens, drawing mention in the narratives of both of the historians Thucydides and Xenophon.[44] Exiled from Rhodes during the war, Dorieus ended up in a new settlement called Thurii, in Italy, and continued to fight against Athens as a naval commander. When two of his ships were captured, Dorieus was brought to Athens. Although he had been condemned to death, when the people of Athens saw Dorieus, they set him free without demanding a ransom.[45] Such was the status and reputation of the athlete and his family.

The success of Diagoras's family stretched into a third generation. Two of Diagoras's grandsons won Olympian crowns in boxing—Eucles and Peisirodus. Callipateira (or, perhaps, Pherenice), the daughter of Diagoras and the mother of Peisirodus, is one of the few notable female names to have survived from accounts of the Olympian festival. Pausanias explains that Callipateira's husband had died, and she was anxious to watch her son compete at Olympia, so she disguised herself as his trainer. When Peisirodus was victorious in the final bout, she jumped over the barrier that separated the trainers from the athletes. Pausanias discreetly, yet clearly, indicates that, as she jumped over the barrier, Callipateira's clothing was stripped away, and she was discovered to be a woman. The laws of Elis indicated that any women caught present at the Olympian Games or in the Olympian sanctuary during the festival were to be thrown to their deaths from the heights of Mount Typaeum, a nearby mountain with high, dangerous cliffs. Although this is the penalty that should have awaited Callipateira, the Olympian officials declined to punish her out of respect for the Olympian achievements of her son, her brothers, and her father. One imagines that

Callipateira herself knew a thing or two about boxing, and perhaps her own fighting prowess, along with the reputations of her father, brothers, and son, was a reason the Olympian officials hesitated to decide to mete out a punishment for her transgression. At any rate, Pausanias tells us, this is the reason that athletic trainers were subsequently required to strip naked at the games.[46]

Female Athletes and Champions in the Crown Games

The story of Callipateira at Olympia is remarkable for several reasons. For hundreds of years, females were almost systematically excluded from the Crown Games, with a few exceptions for priestesses and, perhaps, unmarried girls. Pausanias is quite clear that unmarried girls (*parthenoi*) were not shut out from watching the events in the stadium at Olympia.[47] Matthew Dillon has argued persuasively that the rule forbidding women from the games at Olympia applied only to married, adult females. Unmarried girls, as Pausanias states, were allowed to watch, just as unmarried girls were allowed to compete at Olympia in the Heraia festival.[48] Even so, we have very few names of females who actually attended the Olympian festival and no surviving names of girls who competed in the Heraia. Indeed, even the name of Callipateira was disputed in antiquity, as she was sometimes referred to as Pherenice.

The Spartan princess Cynisca was the first woman to win a victory at Olympia, but she was not allowed to attend the competition. Rather, Cynisca was the owner of the four-horse chariots that won in 396 BCE and 392 BCE. Archaeology has revealed the base of her victory statue and the dedicatory epigram boldly proclaimed her status as a female Olympian victor. After giving her name, her city, and the event she won, Cynisca concludes her epigram, "I assert that I am the only woman in all of Greece to have won the crown."[49] Pausanias relates that, after Cynisca, other women, especially Spartan women, won Olympian victories in the equestrian events, but none was more distinguished than Cynisca.[50] Belistiche, a Macedonian woman, won an Olympian victory with a chariot pulled by a pair of colts around the year 264 BCE.[51] Berenice, a Ptolemaic queen in Egypt, competed in several Crown Games events and won a victory in the Isthmian Games, earning her the right to an epinician poem composed by the famed poet Callimachus.[52] Other women from the Ptolemaic kingdom's royal family were also recognized as victors in the Crown Games (more on them below).

Athletic competitions for females seem to have developed in the first century CE at the Pythian, Nemean, and Isthmian Games but not at Olympia. A set of inscriptions recovered at Delphi commemorates the daughters of Hermesianax, a first-century-CE citizen of both Athens and Delphi. These inscriptions reveal that a daughter named Tryphosa won a stade race at the Pythian Games, and her sister Hedea won a chariot race at Isthmia, a stade race at Nemea, and a music competition at Athens. Dionysia, the third daughter, won a stade race at Isthmia as well as other Panhellenic events.[53] The details of these competitions remain frustratingly obscure. It seems unlikely that these females competed as lone females in traditionally male events. Rather, the most plausible scenario would be a female-oriented festival akin to the Heraia at Olympia. Pausanias indicates that women from Athens, called Thyiads, journeyed to Dephi every year to worship Dionysus, performing dances along the way. Along with the women of Delphi, these pilgrims participated in "mysterious rites" for Dionysus, but no further details are known.[54] Without additional names, sources, or information, the particulars of these festivals, rituals, and competitions for females will remain unknown. Even though the Hermesianax inscription represents some of the best evidence for female participation in athletic contests, it seems to raise more questions than it answers.

Politics, Tyrants, Rulers, and Victory by Association

The reputation that came with a victory in the Crown Games could bring a considerable amount of prestige and authority to an ancient Greek athlete. Rulers, tyrants, and leaders in the ancient Greek world often sought to associate themselves with athletic victory.[55] The *kleos* gained through association would enhance their prestige while allowing them to avoid the possible embarrassment of defeat. In the sixth century BCE, Cimon, a three-time Olympian victor in chariot races, "gave" his second victory to the Athenian tyrant Peisistratus.[56] In the early fourth century BCE, Aristonous, a six-time Pythian champion in kithara singing, offered to transfer his next victory to the Spartan military commander Lysander.[57] In both of these instances, a prominent ruler of leader could claim prestige and justify his authority through a vicarious victory. As with presiding and sponsoring games or entering equestrian events, this type of association with athletic victory allowed tyrants, rulers, and leaders to tap into the exalting power of victory with no risk of defeat.[58]

In 416 BCE, the Athenian Alcibiades earned unprecedented success in the Olympian Games when he entered seven teams into the four-horse chariot race, winning first, second, and fourth places (one of the few times the records note any finishers other than the winner of an event). Alcibiades used his success at Olympia to lobby the Athenians for the right to command their ill-fated expedition to Sicily in 415. The historian Thucydides, a contemporary of Alcibiades, relates that some Athenians saw Alcibiades's actions as a chariot-race competitor and his claims to military authority as signs of an intention to seize power at Athens as a tyrant.[59] Although Alcibiades never seized control of Athens, the connection between athletic victory and political authority remained strong throughout the Archaic, Classical, and Hellenistic eras.

Another case is a negative example, where a ruler refused to augment his prestige and authority by associating himself with a Crown Games festival. In 390 BCE, the Spartan king Agesilaus declined to preside over the Isthmian Games while he was campaigning near Corinth. The Spartan king and his army were in the midst of a long war against the Corinthians, Athenians, and Argives. Civil war in Corinth had driven many pro-Spartan Corinthians into the Spartan camp as exiles, and together they began to campaign against Argive-controlled Corinth. As Agesilaus and his army approached the isthmus, the Argives were in the process of celebrating the Isthmian Games. Frightened by the arrival of a hostile Spartan army, they fled back to Corinth, leaving all the preparations for the festival and games as they were at Isthmia. Instead of pursuing the Corinthians and their allies, Agesilaus camped at Isthmia, observed the sacrifices, and allowed the Corinthian exiles to conduct the Isthmian Games. The Corinthian exiles begged Agesilaus to oversee the games, an honor he declined, preferring instead to stay close with his army and offer protection from the Argives. After the games were concluded and the Spartans left the isthmus, the Argives came out of Corinth and held the Isthmian Games all over again.[60] This episode demonstrates the importance of controlling and presiding over the Crown Games for the Greeks, an importance especially evident in Agesilaus's admonishment of the Argives who had abandoned the sanctuary to his army. They considered presiding over the Isthmian Games a great honor, he remarked, but they had cowardly refused to fight to maintain that honor.[61]

Later in the fourth century BCE, presiding over the games became a much more common occurrence for kings and tyrants who wished to emphasize their reputations. Jason of Pherae, the leader (*tagos*) of the region of Thessaly, planned to preside over and supervise the Pythian Games of 370 BCE before he was assassinated.[62] Philip II of Macedon, the father of Alexander the Great, exercised nearly exclusive control over the Delphic Amphictyony and was awarded the right to administer the Pythian Games in the 340s.[63] In 290 BCE, the Macedonian ruler Demetrius Poliorcetes was unwilling to travel to Delphi for the Pythian Games since his enemies controlled the routes into the mountainous region. Instead, Demetrius decided to preside over an alternative version of the Pythian Games at Athens, declaring that this was appropriate since the Athenians worshiped Apollo as well.[64]

In addition to presiding over the Crown Games, the possibilities presented by a Panhellenic audience were not lost on the kings and rulers of the Greek and Hellenistic worlds. As previously mentioned, Alexander's Exiles Decree was read at the Olympian Games of 324 BCE, and the Roman Flamininus declared "freedom and autonomy" for the Greeks at the Isthmian Games of 196 BCE. There is a suggestion that one Hellenistic king read his own work to the Panhellenic crowd at one of the Crown Games festivals. Historian Timothy Howe has argued persuasively that the Macedonian dynast Ptolemy I, a general who served under Philip II and Alexander the Great, presided over the Isthmian Games of 308 BCE while he was trying to drum up support from the Greeks during the upheavals that wracked the Greek world in the years after Alexander's death in 323 BCE.[65] Ptolemy's horses were victorious in the two-horse chariot race at the Pythian Games of 314 BCE, but it was his role in the games at Isthmia that helped to cement his rule as the Macedonian king of Egypt.[66]

After the death of Alexander the Great in 323 BCE, many of his leading military commanders began to stake their claims to portions of the territory he had conquered as they vied with one another for power. Eventually, Ptolemy I gained control of Egypt and began to exert influence on mainland Greece. In 308 BCE, Ptolemy was in control of Corinth and conceivably presided at the Isthmian Games. According to Howe, the Isthmian Games would have presented an appealing and ideal venue for Ptolemy to read and publicize his *History of Alexander*, an important eyewitness account of Alexander's campaigns that has since been lost.[67] The Panhellenic nature of the Isthmian Games would have provided an effective and useful means of disseminating Ptolemy's message of "Hellenic triumph" to the Greek world in his own bid to augment his authority and to reconstitute Alexander's empire. Ptolemy's enthusiasm for the Crown Games continued on through his descendants, especially the women in the ruling family.

In 2001, a collection of 112 Hellenistic epigrams (or short metrical poetic compositions) was published for the first time after being discovered on a papyrus scroll from ancient Egypt. This collection is attributed to a third-century-BCE poet named Posidippus of Pella and includes a section dedicated to victors in the equestrian events, many of whom were nobles and royals from Ptolemaic Egypt.[68] As historian Sofie Remijsen has demonstrated, the epigrams suggest that the Ptolemaic family dominated the four-horse chariot competitions at Olympia during the first half of the third century BCE. The ruling Ptolemy family also experienced success in the equestrian events at the other Crown Games. The epigrams reveal that horses belonging to one Ptolemaic princess named Berenice won all of the chariot races one year at the Nemean Games.[69] One epigram describes the Ptolemaic ruling family as *aethlophorous*, or "prize bearers," suggesting wide-ranging victories beyond the Crown Games.[70] Another epigram boasts of a winner's greatness from the point of view of the victorious horses. Honoring their owner, the horses proclaim that they have brought *kleos* to Berenice, and they have "seized the long-lasting glory of Cynisca of Sparta."[71] Clearly, female chariot owners felt the rivalry of competition and experienced the glory of victory in the Crown Games, albeit from a distance. It is evident that their participation in the Panhellenic Crown Games offered a powerful occasion for the Ptolemies to claim and reinforce their status as Greeks and dynasts in their drive to maintain and extend their rule in Egypt and elsewhere.

Although Ptolemy I and his successors were ultimately unable to reconstruct Alexander's conquests, the dynasty's rulers controlled Egypt for nearly three hundred years, surrendering its leadership only when Cleopatra VII used a snakebite to end her own life as the Romans closed in. As Howe notes, "At the Isthmian Games, everything seemed possible" in 308 BCE for the aspiring Ptolemy I as he attempted to capitalize on his associations with Alexander in a Panhellenic venue imbued with the power of struggle and victory.[72] The Ptolemaic ruling family continued its associations with the Crown Games as they sought to burnish their image and extend their influence.

In addition to presiding over the games and using them to make announcements and proclamations, rulers and leaders of the ancient Greek world tried to associate themselves with successful athletes in an effort to boost their own reputations. During the early fourth century BCE, the runner Dicon reportedly won five times at Delphi, three times at Olympia, four at Nemea, and three at Isthmia. Pausanias indicates that this outstanding runner had as many statues at Olympia as races he had won (presumably, this referred to his victories in Olympian races). Although he was from a town called Caulonia, a Greek city-state situated near the "toe" of the boot of Italy, his victories caught the eye of Dionysius, the tyrant of Syracuse, on the island of Sicily just across the Strait of Messina from Caulonia. Under Dionysius's patronage, Dicon accepted a payment (or bribe) to change his citizenship to the city of Syracuse, allowing the tyrant and his city to bask in Dicon's reflected glory.[73]

That Dionysius of Syracuse wanted to associate himself with such a renowned athlete as Dicon is no surprise. A hundred years earlier, the tyrants that ruled much of Sicily had recognized the political importance of victory in the Crown Games, and a Syracusan named Hiero, brother of the tyrant Gelo, had won equestrian victories at Olympia and Delphi. Subsequently, he had erected statues at Olympia and commissioned the poets Pindar and Bacchylides to commemorate his equestrian victories. These commemorations survive today as Pindar's *Olympian* 1 and *Pythian*s 1 and 2 and Bacchylides's Ode 3 and Ode 5.[74] Polyzalus, another tyrant on the island, dedicated the Charioteer bronze statue at Delphi around 470 BCE, and this remains today the only bronze athletic-victory statue recovered from a Crown Games site.[75] A hundred years later, the Syracusan Dionysius I also tried to capitalize on Crown Games victory to augment his authority as a tyrant in Sicily with his offer to Dicon.

Dionysius I was one of the more successful Greek tyrants in the years after the Peloponnesian War (ended 404 BCE). After seizing power in Syracuse, he managed to consolidate control over the eastern portion of Sicily and some parts of the Italian mainland. Like other rulers, Dionysius routinely surrounded himself with notable artists, athletes, and intellectuals of the fifth and fourth centuries BCE, and Dicon's acceptance of Syracusan citizenship is consistent with Dionysius's attempts to augment his court with radiated *kleos* and prestige.

Unlike the earlier tyrants of Syracuse, however, Dionysius was unsuccessful in his pursuit of winning Olympian *kleos* in his own right. The ancient historian Diodorus Siculus relates that in 388 BCE Dionysius sent several teams of horses to Olympia to compete in the four-horse chariot event, and these magnificent teams were decked out with all sorts of expensive finery and trappings. In addition to his equestrian entries, Dionysius sent along talented rhapsodes, or poetic performers, whom he'd hired to perform at Olympia the poetry that he had himself composed. Although the rhapsodes initially gathered an impressive crowd at Olympia with their pleasing voices, the listeners soon realized that the poetry itself was very poor, and they began to boo and harass the performers. Some in the crowd, Diodorus tells us, were so unruly that they plundered the entourage's tents. Dionysius's bad luck did not end there. Apparently, his teams of chariots crashed badly during the races, and the delegation's ship was wrecked on its return from Olympia.[76]

This was likely the context when a young boxer named Antipater of Miletus spurned the offer of Dionysius's representatives at Olympia. Pausanias relates that, as they had with Dicon, the Syracusans offered the young athlete a bribe to switch over his citizenship, an offer which the boy refused. The inscription on his victory statue proudly proclaimed his Milesian heritage, a direct repudiation of Dionysius's attempt to buy Olympian prestige rather than earn it himself.[77] Although the rulers and leaders of the Greek world did their best to associate themselves with Crown Games competitions and glory, in the end, the glory of victory was difficult to buy, manufacture, or appropriate. Athletes had to earn it for themselves.

CHAPTER 7

Conclusions

Future Directions for Investigating the Crown Games

If an athlete was competing at Olympia . . . , you would expect him to be both noble and good, and—by Zeus—if he were going to the Pythian or Nemean Games, you would expect him to take care of his body, since the contests are public and popular.

—PHILOSTRATUS, *APOLLONIUS OF TYANA* 35.3

The grandeur and dignity of [Olympic] processions and attitudes, the impressive splendour of ceremonies, the concurrence of all the arts, popular emotion and generous sentiment, must all in some sort collaborate together. . . . It is possible to draw inspiration from the past without copying it.

—PIERRE DE COUBERTIN, FOUNDER OF THE INTERNATIONAL OLYMPIC COMMITTEE, "WHY I REVIVED THE OLYMPIC GAMES," TRANS. HELEN CHISHOLM

What did the Crown Games mean to the ancient Greeks? What did they represent to those who competed, to those who attended, and to those back home who only heard the stories of the splendor of the sanctuaries and the feats of the athletic champions? From the early sixth century BCE up to the late fourth century CE, the Crown Games were regularly celebrated to honor the gods and to identify individuals of outstanding physical ability, skill, and *arete*. For hundreds of years, the Crown Games acted as integral features of Panhellenic sanctuaries that allowed Greeks to cultivate some sense, albeit limited, of Panhellenic identity, and individuals to gain and to advertise their individual glory. Few things in recorded history, let alone in ancient Greece, have enjoyed the chronological continuity and stability of the Crown Games. Although the games at Isthmia and Nemea suffered considerable disruptions—Isthmia suffering from the cataclysmic destruction of Corinth in 146 BCE, and the Nemean Games were moved to the city of Argos—the overall arc of the Crown Games festivals is one of continuity. Wars, plagues, and natural disasters did little to interrupt the festival circuit. Although the sanctuaries where the games took place welcomed Greeks from all over the Mediterranean world, rivalries among the city-states that administered the games ran deep as the cities competed with one another in augmenting the prestige of their respective festivals.

Herodotus alludes to unfair officiating among the Eleans, who administered the Olympian festival, when he records the (probably invented) story of Elean officials visiting ancient Egypt. Herodotus tells us that the Eleans asked the Egyptians, considered the wisest of ancient peoples, for advice on how to make their rules and administration of the Olympian festival as fair as possible. When the Egyptians learned that Elean athletes competed in the contests, they chided the Eleans since Elean judges would tend to favor their fellow citizens.[1] In at least one recorded instance, this seems to have happened, when a Greek runner named Eupolemus of Elis was unfairly awarded a victory in the stade race at Olympia by his hometown judges in the 390s BCE. Although the judges were fined for their verdict, Eupolemus was remembered as the victor in the records preserved by later historians, and he augmented his Olympian crown with pentathlon victories at Delphi and Nemea.[2] Despite the admonitions of the Egyptians, Elean athletes continued to participate at Olympia, as did Argives at the Nemean Games, Corinthians at the Isthmian Games, and citizens of Delphi at the Pythian Games.

The wrangling and politicking that went into preparing, overseeing, judging, and otherwise administering the Crown Games was as ingrained as the divisions among the various Greek city-states. Owing to the prestige that came from administering these great festivals, there are several examples of cities vying with one another for the right to do so.

Perhaps no story illustrates the fierce rivalry for control over Olympia better than the battle fought there in 364 BCE.

Xenophon and the Battle in the Altis of 364 BCE

Xenophon, a historian from the fourth century BCE, describes in his work the turbulent times of the Greek world after the end of the Peloponnesian War in 404 BCE but before the Macedonian conquest of 338 BCE. While the Greek city-states of this time formed and dissolved alliances as they vied with one another for supremacy, Xenophon tells in book 7 of his *Hellenica* how two groups of Greeks—the Arcadians and Eleans—squared off in a series of battles in the fourth century BCE.

In 365 BCE, the people of Elis seized the city of Lasion (modern Lalas), a small settlement that had once been in their territory but was then controlled by a conglomerate of allied cities called the Arcadian League.[3] The large Arcadian League army, however, quickly regained Lasion and extended its counteroffensive into Elean territory, capturing the sanctuary of Olympia and building a defensive fortification there around the hill of Kronos.[4]

The next year—364 BCE—was the year for an Olympian festival. Xenophon continues his narrative, relating that the Arcadians strengthened their fortifications at Olympia and prepared to celebrate the Olympian Games. However, since the Arcadians were at war with the people of Elis, the Arcadians enlisted the help of the people of Pisa, a nearby town that, in the distant past, had possessed the right to oversee the Olympian Games before the larger city of Elis had taken charge. The Eleans, on the other hand, openly prepared to hold the Olympian Games themselves, and on the designated day, their sacred procession left Elis and headed out along the road to Olympia, accompanied by their allies.

The Arcadians and the Pisans did not anticipate the Eleans and their allies coming to Olympia during the athletic program, and they had already begun the athletic competitions when the Eleans drew near. The horse racing was finished, and the pentathlon was underway. The "stadium" events of the pentathlon were already done, and those athletes who had reached the wrestling stage were no longer in the stadium but had moved into the Altis, near the altar of Zeus.

As the Eleans approached, the Arcadian soldiers scrambled to defend the sanctuary. The Arcadians formed a defensive battle line on the west side of the sanctuary, along the Cladeus River, and the Eleans drew up across from them. Although the Eleans had no strong reputation in warfare, that day they fought with uncharacteristic valor. They crossed the river and defeated the Arcadians in a pitched battle and then defeated the reinforcements that rushed to the line.

However, Xenophon continues, when the Eleans reached the area between the Bouleuterion and the Temple of Hestia and the adjoining theater, their progress slowed. Although they continued to drive the enemy toward the great altar of Zeus, they were pelted by projectiles from enemies atop the stoae, the Bouleuterion, and the great Temple of Zeus. When Stratolas, the leader of a picked group of Eleans (called the Three Hundred), was killed, the Eleans retired back to their own encampment, presumably back across the Cladeus River.

With the Eleans withdrawn across the Cladeus River, the Arcadians stayed up all night dismantling the elaborately constructed tents and booths and using those materials to build a defensive barrier. When the Elean soldiers returned the next day and saw the strong wall and the armed men who had climbed on top of the temples, ready to defend the sanctuary, the Eleans went back to their city, having demonstrated *arete* in a way that only a god like Zeus can inspire.[5]

This remarkable account raises several questions concerning the organization and the administration of the ancient Olympian festival. First off, as the Eleans arrived near the sanctuary at Olympia, the wrestling component of the pentathlon was taking place not inside the stadium, as we might expect, but in the Altis, near the altar of Zeus. Typical modern treatments of ancient sport place all of the athletic competitions, except for the equestrian events, in the stadium, and practical considerations make this the best possible venue.[6] There are a few possible explanations for Xenophon's divergence from what we might expect, and none of them is entirely satisfactory. Perhaps the wrestlers were in the Altis during this particular festival because of the heightened danger and the state of war. Perhaps there was an area in the Altis where wrestling events always took place, and the ancient sources have obscured the details (archaeology suggests no such potential location). Or perhaps Xenophon invented this detail to make sure that there were adequate numbers of spectators inside the Altis to pelt the encroaching Eleans from the rooftops of the temples. What seems unlikely is that Xenophon simply made a mistake about how Olympia was organized and how the Olympian festival was run. Certainly, Xenophon was familiar with the layout of the sanctuary at Olympia. He lived just across the

Alpheus River. While he was in exile from Athens, the Spartans gave him land in Scillus, a small village near the sanctuary of Olympia, south of the Alpheus River. In addition, Xenophon at his own expense founded a nearby shrine to Artemis that was located only twenty stade lengths—less than three miles—from the Temple of Zeus at Olympia.[7] Surely, he knew the area of Olympia well.

Even more puzzling than the reported site of the pentathlon wrestling is Xenophon's description of the battle's progression, where the Eleans pushed the Arcadians into the space "between the Bouleuterion and the Temple of Hestia and the adjoining theater."[8] As noted in the chapter on Olympia, archaeological excavations uncovered the remnants of the Bouleuterion in the nineteenth century along the southern side of the Altis. The locations of the Temple of Hestia and the theater, however, are not forthcoming. Xenophon's version of the battle is incompatible with the location of the Bouleuterion on the southern edge of the Altis near the Alpheus River. There is no theater or Temple of Hestia nearby, nor are there any potentially persuasive candidates. Clearly, something is amiss in this story. Where might the Temple of Hestia and the theater at Olympia be?

The goddess Hestia was often worshiped in conjunction with political institutions and civic buildings rather than with religious ones.[9] Typically, Hestia was the goddess of the hearth, and her worship centered around a public fireplace. There are attested temples or sanctuaries of Hestia in ancient Greece, but Xenophon's account seems to be the only attestation of a freestanding structure at Olympia dedicated to this goddess. Pausanias fails to mention this temple in his description of Olympia, but his account is not comprehensive. An altar to Hestia often featured prominently in a different type of ancient Greek building called a *prytaneion*. Typically, a *prytaneion* featured dining halls for official guests of the state, archives of laws or other important documents, historical artifacts, and a ceremonial hearth with a perpetual fire dedicated to Hestia. As Stephen G. Miller has phrased it, the *prytaneion* "symbolized the life of the city."[10] Olympia's *prytaneion* was situated near the Temple of Hera, an excavated site that corresponds to the location described by Pausanias.[11] Judging by the proximity of this building to the Cladeus River and the civic function of both the Prytaneion and the Bouleuterion, it seems likely that Xenophon meant the Prytaneion (not the Bouleuterion) and its "shrine" to Hestia as the site for the Battle in the Altis. Stephen G. Miller has argued forcefully and compellingly for this version of the battle's geography.[12] Even if we can accept this substitution of the Prytaneion for the Bouleuterion in Xenophon's account, there is one more building to account for—the theater.

A Theater at Olympia?

Where was the theater of ancient Olympia, and what exactly was it used for? Archaeology has not (yet) revealed a theater structure at Olympia, nor does Pausanias mention one in his description, but this is not cause to doubt its existence. Passing references to the theater at Olympia crop up in several literary and epigraphic sources. A corpus of inscriptions indicates that during the third century BCE, a growing field of professional actors organized themselves into guilds and performed regularly at the Crown Games sites, as well as at other locations in the Hellenistic Greek world. One of the most prominent of these guilds called itself the Isthmian-Nemean guild, and it was firmly in place by the middle of the third century (i.e., the 250s BCE).[13] It seems safe to assume, based on its name, that the guild participated in dramatic contests or events at the Crown Games sites of Isthmia and Nemea, and multiple inscriptions attest to the guild's relationship with the officials at Delphi. The theater at Delphi was prominently situated near the Temple of Apollo, and the theater at Isthmia was near the Temple of Poseidon. No ancient theater survives in ancient Nemea, but Argos, which hosted the Nemean Games for much of their history, certainly featured one since it is mentioned in literary sources.[14] However, the theater at Olympia is missing.

In the chapter on Isthmia, we encountered the inscription honoring the chorus leader Pythocles and his thirteen victories at Nemea, Isthmia, Delphi, and—if the restoration is correct—three more at Olympia (the number won at Olympia, not the name of the site, is uncertain because of the corrupted text).[15] While it seems unlikely that these dramatic contests earned reputation and renown on par with the gymnastic and equestrian events, the few surviving victory monuments of this type indicate that the victors took a considerable amount of pride in a Crown Games victory in drama. When these dramatic contests at Olympia might have been held is difficult to determine. Philostratus, a late source, writes that Delphi offered its visitors musical and dramatic events before the gymnastic events took place, while at Olympia there were only the gymnastics.[16] Perhaps the dramatic contests took place at a different time than the Olympian festival or perhaps not at all. The literary sources are quite convincing, though, that performances were a regular part of the Olympian experience and that—at some point in time—these took place in a theater.

Ancient literary sources describe a litany of performance activities that took place during the Crown Games festivals. The Roman-era sophist Lucian writes that Herodotus (a fifth-century-BCE figure) took advantage of the assemblage at the Olympian Games to deliver his *Histories* to an admiring crowd from the back porch of the Temple of Zeus (an area called the opisthodomos). Although Lucian is surely describing his own time rather than the time of Herodotus during the fifth century BCE (when the Temple of Zeus at Olympia was yet under construction), Lucian indicates that Herodotus's example sparked a long litany of rhetorical and sophistic performances at Olympia.[17] Although the details of Lucian's account appear to be invented, there are historical records of other notable rhetorical performances at Olympia. Olympian speeches by the sophists and rhetoricians Gorgias, Lysias, and Isocrates have survived, at least in fragmentary form, and these three took advantage of the Panhellenic crowds gathered for the games to urge the Greeks to unify in the face of their endemic strife and discord.[18]

As related earlier, around the year 400 BCE, the Sicilian tyrant Dionysius I hired professionals to perform his original poetry at Olympia—and the verses were so bad that the crowd booed and harassed the performers.[19] Lucian also provides us with an eyewitness account of the strange tale of Peregrinus, a philosopher turned Christian turned back to philosopher, who made elaborate and public plans to immolate himself very close to the theater at Olympia. In the end Peregrinus burned himself to death a couple of miles away from the sanctuary after the Olympian Games had concluded, to Lucian's scathing ridicule.[20]

Although Lucian indicates that the opisthodomos of the Temple of Zeus was a favorite spot for speech givers at Olympia in his time, there must have been a theater for the dramatic performances that dated to at least the third century BCE. Judith Barringer has noted that a theater in the Greek world during the time of Xenophon was often a temporary structure with benches on three sides of a rectangle. She suggests that a temporary theater might have been situated in the southeast corner of the Altis, near the Bouleuterion, for spectators to watch victorious athletes receive their crowns in. The logic is appealing because it validates Xenophon's account to some extent (placing Hestia's temple in the southeast corner of the Altis). It also seems feasible to have fit a temporary theater into the Altis before the construction of the Temple of Zeus in the mid-fifth century BCE. The problem with this argument, though, is trying to understand how a theater fitting thousands of spectators could have fit into the Altis of Xenophon's time during the early fourth century—an Altis that featured a massive Temple of Zeus and was also crammed with victory monuments, athlete statues, and the tents and structures described in Xenophon's account. Barringer's scenario is not impossible, but it is difficult to imagine.[21] One other possibility emerges: ancient Greek theaters typically took advantage of nearby terrain, and the best natural site at Olympia for a theater is the southwestern slope of the hill of Kronos, on the west side of the sanctuary, at a site near the Prytaneion and its hearth to Hestia. Until more evidence emerges, the search for Olympia's theater will continue.

Conclusion

While the sacrifices and athletic contests of the Olympian festival clearly held precedence among the ancient Greek pilgrims and priests, there was evidently much more going on at the ancient Olympian festival. Similar complexities presumably existed at the other Crown Games sites. Delphi, especially, enjoyed a formidable reputation as the navel of the world and the seat of the Amphictyony. Despite the immense strides made in the past 150 years by archaeologists, historians, art historians, classicists, kinesiologists, and other scholars, the Battle in the Altis in 364 BCE reminds us just how fragile and tenuous our knowledge of Olympia is. In addition, we are reminded how modern treatments of the Olympian festival are heavily dependent on modern ideals of what athletic festivals should include. Rhetorical performances, philosophical posturing, and dramatic competitions in the unlocated theater show up in our evidence but are largely absent from our discussions of the ancient Olympian festival. Modern definitions and expectations of athletic competitions, as well as the rise of the modern Olympic Games, inform our examination of the ancient festivals. However, the modern world is not solely to blame. Another reason for the dismissal of these Crown Games features and events is a heavy reliance on Pausanias, who declined to comment on the dedications of musical competitors. Even at Delphi, where the Pythian Games held the most prominent musical contests of those at all the Crown Games sites, Pausanias dismissed the musical champions as obscure.[22]

Pausanias relates that, around 350 years after the Battle in the Altis, during repairs to the roof of the Temple of Hera in the Altis, the workers discovered the corpse of a soldier who had died from wounds suffered in battle. Although Pausanias assigns this soldier to a different war, it seems clear enough that this soldier died during the Battle in the Altis of 364 BCE.[23] Apparently, this unfortunate dead man was among those who climbed atop the Temple of Hera to defend the sanctuary, where he lost consciousness from his wounds and slipped into a gap in the temple eaves, to be discovered over 300 years later. Pausanias tells us that the man was buried, still wearing his armor, outside of the Altis at Olympia.[24] Just as that unfortunate soldier perished in the eaves of the Temple of Hera at Olympia and remained there for 350 years, much of what happened in conjunction with the Olympian festival still remains hidden from view, waiting, perhaps, for modern investigators to unearth it. With continued research, attention to detail, and a comprehensive approach to all sources, not only those focused on the events that correlate with modern athletics, perhaps we can continue to uncover these hidden pieces of the Olympian past.

The Crown Games ended in the fourth century CE with the conversion of the Roman Empire to Christianity. The temples were closed, the sacrificial fires were extinguished, looters robbed the statues and the treasures, the sanctuaries fell into disrepair, and the memory of the Crown Games faded into obscurity. In later years, the periodic revival of Olympic festivals resurrected the idea of ancient Olympia in the modern world, but this was a far cry from the ancient Panhellenic circuit of the Crown Games. Indeed, with the institution of the current version of the Olympic Games in 1896 at Athens, the idea of Olympia has become definitively divorced from its geographic location. In 1996, Stephen G. Miller led a revival of the Nemean Games, dubbed the "New Nemean Games," at Nemea. This modern version of the Nemean Games occurs every four years (instead of biennially), women are allowed to participate in it, its athletes compete in robes (called chitons), and it has grown in popularity since the revival.[25] Yet aside from the hordes of tourists that crowd Olympia each summer, the Crown Games as a historical circuit go largely unremarked in present times.

Visitors to Olympia sense the importance of the site and often converse with one another in reverent tones while they wander about the toppled columns and foundation stones in the ruined sanctuary. Delphi still welcomes busloads of pilgrims seeking the navel of the world and the natural beauty of Apollo's prophetic seat on Parnassus, but relatively few visitors exert the effort to climb all the way to the stadium at the top of the sanctuary or to descend past the Castalian Spring to the gymnasium in the lower sanctuary. The site of Nemea enjoys frequent visits from busloads of schoolchildren, but even in Pausanias's time the Temple of Zeus was decrepit and abandoned. Isthmia is nestled along a quiet stretch of seashore on the Saronic Gulf, and the sea breeze that rustles through the pine trees hardly compares to the din and clamor associated with the philosophic rantings of Diogenes the Cynic. The treasuries and temples lie in ruins, barely more than foundations, and most of the myriad victory statues, inscriptions, and dedicatory offerings have long been looted and plundered from the sites. It is difficult for visitors today to imagine the solemnity of the sacrifices, the pounding excitement of galloping horses in the hippodromes, the haunting musical performances at Delphi, the crunch of a hardened fist breaking a boxer's nose, the breathless sprinting of pentathletes, and the roar of the crowd as a Crown Games winner showed his *arete* and earned his *kleos*. It is difficult, but not impossible, to sense the deep-rooted quest for *kleos* and *arete*, the striving for immortal honors, and the drive for athletic victory that marked these sites for hundreds of years.

NOTES

Author's Preface

1. BCE, an abbreviation for "before the Common Era," is synonymous with BC (before Christ). The equivalent to AD (Anno Domini) is CE (Common Era). Scholarship in ancient history conventionally uses BCE and CE for dates. No religious or secular agenda is implied by their use in this book.
2. There are many commentaries on and treatments of Pausanias, the most famous perhaps being the six-volume nineteenth-century translation and commentary of Sir James Frazer (Cambridge: Cambridge University Press, 2012). More recent treatments include Christian Habicht's *Pausanias' Guide to Ancient Greece* (Berkeley: University of California Press, 1985) and William Hutton's *Describing Greece: Landscape and Literature in the* Periegesis *of Pausanias* (Cambridge: Cambridge University Press, 2005).
3. Pausanias 6.3.8.

Introduction

1. For detailed examinations of the role of athletics in ancient Greek civic life, see Paul Christesen, *Sport and Democracy in the Ancient and Modern Worlds* (Cambridge: Cambridge University Press, 2012); Nigel Kennell, *The Gymnasium of Virtue: Education and Culture in Ancient Sparta* (Chapel Hill: University of North Carolina Press, 1995); Donald G. Kyle, *Athletics in Ancient Athens* (Leiden, Netherlands: E. J. Brill, 1987); and David M. Pritchard, *Sport, Democracy and War in Classical Athens* (Cambridge: Cambridge University Press, 2013).
2. Plutarch, *Life of Solon* 23, indicates that, under the laws of Solon, Athenian victors at Olympia received 500 drachmas, and victors at Isthmia could claim 100. While victors in the Crown Games often could count on lucrative rewards from their cities, the timing of the particular episode described here is suspect since Solon was archon at Athens in the 590s BCE—before the institution of the Panhellenic Crown Games circuit. On the other hand, the writer Diogenes Laertius (1.2.) contended that Solon's reward was actually a *reduction* in the amount of money awarded to victorious athletes at Athens.
3. Stephen G. Miller, *Ancient Greek Athletics* (New Haven, CT: Yale University Press, 2004), 111–12.
4. The Crown Games dial of the Antikythera device is more closely oriented toward our modern calendar with its New Year's Day in January rather than toward a count that begins with a summertime Olympian festival. The Games Dial begins its cycle with the Isthmian festival, held in the spring of year 0 before summertime's Olympian festival. See Myria Anastasiou, Yanis Bitsakis, A. Jones, J. M. Steele, and M. Zafeiropoulou, "The Back Dial and Back Plate

Inscriptions," *Almagest: International Journal for the History of Scientific Ideas* 7, no. 1 (2016): 139–215. The construction of the Antikythera device has been dated only vaguely, with most experts settling on dates between 200 and 100 BCE.

5. Paus. 10.4.2. Plutarch claimed that Delphi belonged as much to Dionysus as to Apollo. Plutarch, *The E at Delphi* 9 (*Moralia* 388E). Michael Scott, *Delphi: A History of the Center of the Ancient World* (Princeton, NJ: Princeton University Press, 2014), 152–53, 220–21. The festivities at Delphi included secret rites to Dionysus as well as a ceremony for young female worshipers of Dionysus. Plutarch, *Isis and Osiris* 35 (*Moralia* 364 E–F).
6. Plutarch, *Life of Aristides* 20.4–5.
7. *NIO* no. 5.
8. Plutarch, *Life of Themistocles* 17.4.
9. Thucydides 3.8.1–3.14.1. The speech of the envoys begins at 3.9.1. The envoys were successful in their endeavor, and Sparta and its allies voted to help the people of Lesbos.
10. Thucydides 5.18.10–11. The peace treaty is called the Peace of Nicias, after an Athenian leader who helped to negotiate it. No pillar was set up at Nemea, presumably because the Nemean Games by this time had been transferred to the nearby city of Argos. In addition, it was around this time (although perhaps after the treaty) that the sanctuary at Nemea was ravaged by warfare (see chap. 3). The omission of Nemea from the treaty sites has led some modern scholars to suggest that Nemea lacked the prestige of the other Crown Games sites. However, Thomas Heine Nielsen has persuasively endeavored to restore the prestige of Nemea in the Crown Games context. See Thomas Heine Nielsen, "The Prestige of a Nemean Victory," pt. 2 in *Two Studies in the History of Ancient Greek Athletics* (Copenhagen: Royal Danish Academy of Sciences and Letters, 2018), 169–229.
11. Thucydides 5.49–50; and Xenophon, *Hellenica* 3.2.21.
12. Sparta would be prevented from sacrificing at Olympia for several years, until about 402 or 401 BCE (the chronology is murky). See Diodorus Siculus 14.17 and 14.34; and Xenophon, *Hellenica* 3.2.26.
13. Thucydides 8.9–10. The Athenians were ready. When the Peloponnesians finally left the isthmus, a group of waiting Athenian ships chased down the Peloponnesian fleet and attacked, disabling most of the Peloponnesian ships and killing the commander.
14. Philostratus, *Lives of the Sophists* 1.9.
15. Gorgias's Olympian speech survives only in fragments and testimonies, and Lysias's "Olympic Oration" (no. 33) is incomplete. Isocrates's speech at Olympia is called "Panegyricus."
16. Diodorus Siculus 18.8.2–6.
17. Herodotus 8.123–124. Herodotus relates that each commander voted for himself as most worthy of the prize, but most of them agreed that Themistocles of Athens was worthy of second place. So, although the debate ended inconclusively, Themistocles was praised widely as the wisest man in Greece. See also Plutarch, *Life of Themistocles* 14, which cites Herodotus as its source.
18. Plutarch, *Life of Philopoemen* 11.1–3.

19. Polybius 18.46.5; Plutarch, *Life of Flamininus* 10; and Peter Green, *Alexander to Actium* (Berkeley: University of California Press, 1990), 311. Plutarch relates that so great was the shout of joy from the assembled Greeks in the stadium at Isthmia that ravens flying overhead fell to the ground because of the disturbance in the air. Of course, Flamininus's proclamation came with some strings attached, and the Romans and Greeks would fight another major war less than thirty years later, resulting in the permanent subjugation of Greece.

Chapter 1

1. Homer, *Odyssey* 8.111–234. After his mighty discus throw, Odysseus boasts to the Phaeacians of his prowess in archery, javelin, boxing, and wrestling but concedes that his running might not be strong, since his many days at sea have prevented suitable training.
2. Hesiod, *Works and Days* 655–59.
3. Walter Burkert, *Greek Religion*, trans. John Raffan (Cambridge, MA: Harvard University Press, 1985), 105. Burkert has traced the idea of "the agonal spirit" of the ancient Greeks to Friedrich Nietzsche, while also identifying plenty of later advocates.
4. Paus. 10.4.1.
5. David Young, *The Olympic Myth of Greek Amateur Athletics* (Chicago: Ares Publishers, 1985), 171.
6. Thomas Heine Nielsen, "A Survey of the Proliferation of Athletic and Equestrian Competitions in Late Archaic and Classical Greece," pt. 1 in *Two Studies*, 11–167; see especially Nielsen's "Catalogue of Agonistic Festivals" on pp. 110–55.
7. Herodotus 5.22. According to the story, Alexander finished his race "equal first," a strange term of uncertain meaning. It is more likely that Alexander I's status as a king allowed him to claim victory than that he actually tied with another runner. For context and commentary, see W. Lindsay Adams, "Other People's Games: The Olympics, Macedonia, and Greek Athletics," *Journal of Sport History* 30, no. 2 (2003): 205–17.
8. Mark Golden, *Sport and Society in Ancient Greece* (Cambridge: Cambridge University Press, 1998), 104–12.
9. Lucian, *Anacharsis* 9–10.
10. Athenaeus 15.674D (*TrGF* 202 and 235).
11. Hyginus, *Poetica astronomica* 2.15.4.
12. Paus. 5.7.7. The olive tree that provided the crowns is mentioned at Paus. 5.15.3.
13. Apollodorus, *Library* 2.5.11. Cf. Pliny, *Natural History* 37.1, which links the origin of wearing rings, a combination of metal and stone, to a commemoration of Prometheus's bondage.
14. Lesile Kurke, "The Economy of Kudos," in *Cultural Poetics in Archaic Greece*, ed. Carol Doughterty and Leslie Kurke (Oxford: Oxford University Press, 1988), 137–42. See Golden, *Sport and Society*, 17–18; and David Sansone, *Greek Athletics and the Genesis of Sport* (Berkeley: University of California Press, 1998), 80–88, for the connections between athletics and sacrifice.

15. Stephen G. Miller, "The Organization and Functioning of the Olympic Games," in *Sport and Festival in the Ancient Greek World*, ed. David Phillips and David Pritchard (Swansea: Classical Press of Wales, 2003), 1–40.
16. The origin of the truce is explained at Paus. 5.4.5–6. Pausanias writes elsewhere (5.20.1) that the words of the truce were inscribed on a dedicated discus at Olympia, although he does not record the text of the inscription. Despite contemporary claims that the ancient Olympian truce instituted universal peace every four years in the Greek world, it is clear that the truce extended only to athletes and pilgrims journeying to the sanctuaries for the occasions of the festivals. See Manfred Lämmer, "The So-Called Olympic Peace in Ancient Greece," in *Greek Athletics*, ed. Jason König (Edinburgh: Edinburgh University Press, 2010), 36–60.
17. Jean Pouilloux, "Travaux à Delphes à l'occasion des Pythia," in "Études delphiques," supplement, *BCH* 4 (1977): 103–23. An English translation is available in Stephen G. Miller, *Arete: Greek Sports from Ancient Sources* (Berkeley: University of California Press, 1991), source no. 81.
18. As the crow flies, Elis is only about thirty-five kilometers from Olympia, but the ancient road wound for fifty-eight kilometers. Miller, "Organization and Functioning," 3.
19. Paus. 5.24.9.
20. Paus. 5.22.1.
21. Mary B. Hollinshead, "'Adyton,' 'Opisthodomos,' and the Inner Room of the Greek Temple," *Hesperia* 68, no. 2 (1999): 189–218.
22. Rod-wielding officials are depicted in several vase paintings and mentioned at Plutarch, *Life of Themistocles* 11, when Themistocles notes the punishment for runners who start too early at the games. Thucydides 5.49–50 mentions the beating administered by the *rhabdouchoi* to Lichas, a Spartan citizen who illegally entered his chariot at Olympia and won.
23. See Miller, "Organization and Functioning," 35n77, on the scantiness of the evidence for such a large sacrificial offering.
24. In particular, Stephen G. Miller's *Ancient Greek Athletics* and Donald G. Kyle's *Sport and Spectacle in the Ancient World* (Malden, MA: Wiley-Blackwell, 2007) offer excellent synopses of ancient Greek athletic culture.
25. Thucydides 1.6.5.
26. Paus. 1.44.1; *IG* VII.52; and Ronald P. Legon, *Megara* (Ithaca, NY: Cornell University Press, 1981), 62–63. The inscription dates from the Roman Empire, and it is possible that Pausanias's claim stemmed from reading this very inscription since Pausanias shares this information in his narrative while describing the tomb of Orsippus at Megara.
27. Plato, *Republic* 452C. Plato notes that the Cretans introduced nude exercise and then the Spartans adopted it, initially incurring ridicule among the rest of the Greeks before they also adopted the practice of exercising naked.
28. David G. Romano, "The Ancient Stadium: Athletes and Arete," *The Ancient World* 7, no. 1–2 (1983): 9–16, explains that the difference between the lengths of stadiums from site to site was connected to the architectural measurements and proportions of each sanctuary's main temple.
29. Posidippus 74. The text, recovered from a fragment of papyrus in Egypt, does

not explain the method of casting lots beyond the fact that each judge cast a short stick to the ground.

30. Paus. 5.8.5–9.2 recounts the addition and subtraction of various events at Olympia.
31. Plutarch, *Life of Themistocles* 5.
32. Xenophon, *Hellenica* 7.4.32.
33. Lysias, *Olympian Oration* 33.2.
34. H. W. Parke, *Festivals of the Athenians* (Ithaca, NY: Cornell University Press, 1977), 19.
35. Burkert, *Greek Religion*, 271.
36. Sansone, *Greek Athletics*, 79.
37. Stephen G. Miller, introduction to *Arete: Greek Sports from Ancient Sources* (Berkeley: University of California Press, 1991), vii.
38. Plato's dialogue *Meno*, for example, starts out with Meno asking Socrates (at 70A) whether *arete* can be taught, whether it can be acquired through practice, or whether it is something that occurs only naturally. Ultimately, the dialogue's characters decide that *arete* neither occurs naturally nor is taught but is best understood as a gift from the gods (99E–100B).
39. Jesper Svenbro, *Phrasikleia: An Anthropology of Reading in Ancient Greece*, trans. Janet Lloyd (Ithaca, NY: Cornell University Press, 1993), 14.
40. Leslie Kurke, *The Traffic in Praise: Pindar and the Poetics of Social Economy* (Ithaca, NY: Cornell University Press, 1991), 17; and Svenbro, *Phrasikleia*, 14–15.
41. Kurke, *Traffic in Praise*, 17. The quotations are from Homer, occurring at *Odyssey* 1.344, 3.83, 3.204, 4.726, 4.816, 19.333, 23.137.
42. Burkert, *Greek Religion,* 203.
43. Hypothesis A to Pindar, *Isthmian*, quoted in Elizabeth Gebhard, "The Beginnings of Panhellenic Games at the Isthmus," in *Olympia 1875–2000: 125 Jahre deutsche Ausgrabungen*, ed. Helmut Kyrieleis (Mainz: Philipp von Zabern, 2002), 221. The comment was written by a scholiast, a term that refers to an anonymous ancient or medieval commentator.

Chapter 2

1. Paus. 5.7.6.
2. Ancient references to an oracle at Olympia include Herodotus 8.134, Strabo 8.3.30, and Pindar, *Olympian* 6.70 (cf. Pindar, *Olympian* 8.2). The precise workings or pronouncements of this oracle are unknown, although Herodotus and Pindar agree that the consultation involved examining the entrails of a sacrificed animal. Strabo indicates that, although the oracle eventually ceased to work, the temple and sanctuary maintained their fame.
3. Recently and compellingly argued by Paul Christesen in "Whence 776? The Origin of the Date for the First Olympiad," in *Sport in the Cultures of the Ancient World: New Perspectives*, ed. Zinon Papakonstantinou (London: Routledge, 2010), 13–34.
4. Paus. 5.10.1. Books 5 and 6 of Pausanias's *Description of Greece* focus on the region of Elis and prominently feature Olympia and its monuments.

5. Helmut Kyrieleis, "The German Excavations at Olympia: An Introduction," in Phillips and Pritchard, *Sport and Festival*, 46–48.
6. Charles Picard, "Les fouilles allemandes au stade d'Olympie et l'histoire des jeux sacrés," *Revue archéologique* 1 (1961): 217.
7. E. Norman Gardiner, *History and Remains of Olympia* (Oxford: Oxford University Press, 1925), 280–81. Excavators recovered an inscription from the site that reads, "Leonidas, [son] of Leotas, of Naxos, built and dedicated [this building] to Olympian Zeus." *IvO* 651. Cf. Paus. 5.15.2, where he seems to have mistakenly identified Leonidas as a local man.
8. Gardiner, *History and Remains*, 217.
9. Gardiner, *History and Remains*, 270–74.
10. Paus. 5.24.9–10. The oath was a prohibition against cheating, literally "that there will be no crimes from them [committed] against the Olympian contests."
11. Paus. 5.6.6.
12. *IvO* 7.
13. See Paus. 5.9.4–6 for the introduction of the *hellanodikai* at Olympia.
14. Paus. 5.14.4–7 indicates that the Altis featured altars to Hestia, Olympian Zeus, Artemis and Athena, Hephaestus, Heracles, and others.
15. Gardiner, *History and Remains*, 206–8.
16. Paus. 5.20.1–2. Pausanias indicates, a bit cryptically, that "on the back" (of the table?) was a list or arrangement of the contests.
17. Callimachus, *Iambus* 6. Paus. 5.11.1–9 describes the statue of Zeus and notes that, although Pausanias knew the statue's measurements, the numbers were unable to describe its magnificence.
18. Strabo, *Geography* 8.3.30. The line from Homer quoted by Pheidias is *Iliad* 1.528.
19. Paus. 5.13.8–10.
20. For a treatment of the various versions of the Pelops myth and their relationships to Olympia, see John Davidson, "Olympia and the Chariot-Race of Pelops," in Phillips and Pritchard, *Sport and Festival*.
21. Pindar, *Olympian* 1.25–27; and Timothy Gantz, *Early Greek Myth* (Baltimore: Johns Hopkins University Press, 1993), 532.
22. See Hygiunus, *Fabula* 84; and Paus. 6.21.9–11 for the names of the unsuccessful and unlucky suitors.
23. See Paus. 6.19.6 for Pelops's dagger and Paus. 5.13.4–6 for the shoulder blade. Pausanias recorded other Pelops relics outside of Olympia, such as the chariot of Pelops at Keleai (2.14.4), his divinely crafted scepter (9.40.11), and his mountain throne at Sipylos (5.13.7). See also Nigel Spivey, *The Ancient Olympics: A History* (Oxford: Oxford University Press, 2004), 215–17.
24. See Paus. 5.10.6–7.
25. See Paus. 5.8.2 for Pelops's holding Olympian Games. See Paus. 5.8.3–4, 5.13.2; and Pindar, *Olympian* 10.24–59 for the Heracles story.
26. Paus. 5.13.1–2.
27. Paus. 6.22.1.
28. Paus. 5.13.1–3.
29. Pindar, *Olympian* 10.24. Heracles as a founder or refounder of the contests at Olympia was a common theme in ancient literature as well—e.g., at Strabo 8.3.33.

30. Helmut Kyrieleis, *Anfänge und Frühzeit des Heiligtums von Olympia: Die Ausgrabungen am Pelopion 1987–1996*, Olympische Forschungen 31 (Berlin: Walter de Gruyter, 2006), 55–61; Kyrieleis, "German Excavations," 52–55; Jörg Rambach, "Olympia: 2500 Jahre Vorgeschichte vor der Gründung des eisenzeitlichen griechischen Heiligtums," in Kyrieleis, *Olympia 1875–2000*, 180–212.
31. Kyrieleis, "German Excavations," 53.
32. Kyrieleis, *Anfänge und Frühzeit*, 55.
33. Alfred Mallwitz, "Cult and Competition Locations at Olympia," in *The Archaeology of the Olympics: The Olympics and Other Festivals in Antiquity*, ed. Wendy J. Raschke (Madison: University of Wisconsin Press, 1988), 102–3. Mallwitz links the expansion of the Olympic festival to Pheidon of Argos, a tyrant who briefly seized control of the games, usually dated to the seventh century BCE.
34. Mallwitz, "Cult and Competition Locations," 94.
35. Mallwitz, "Cult and Competition Locations," 94–95, 99.
36. Eric Brulotte, "The 'Pillar of Oinomaos' and the Location of Stadium I at Olympia," *AJA* 98, no. 1 (1994): 62.
37. Philostratus, *Gymnasticus* 5–6; and Brulotte, "'Pillar of Oinomaos,'" 63. Paus. 5.13.8 explains that the altar of Zeus was situated between the Pelopion and the Temple of Hera but to the east of both of them.
38. Mallwitz, "Cult and Competition Locations," 102–3, considered the location of the altar of Zeus to have been fixed in a general reordering of the sanctuary that he proposed took place around 600 BCE.
39. Paus. 6.20.7.
40. Paus. 5.16.2–8. Thomas Scanlon has investigated the Heraia at length, with perhaps the best synopsis of the scholarship found in his 2002 book *Eros and Greek Athletics* (Oxford: Oxford University Press).
41. Romano, "Ancient Stadium," 9–16.
42. Paus. 5.16.2–6.
43. Paus. 6.20.7, 5.16.4.
44. Scanlon, *Eros and Greek Athletics*, 117–120.
45. Paus. 6.20.9, 5.1.3–4. The winning son was named Epeius, and his descendants reputedly ruled the area until the arrival of Oenomaus. According to Paus. 5.8.6, the first recorded Olympic victor, Koroibos of Elis, was honored with a tomb at the boundary of the region of Elis.
46. Paus. 6.20.10–19 describes the hippodrome, with the Taraxippus treated at 15–19.
47. Elizabeth P. McGowan, "Tomb Marker and Turning Post: Funerary Columns in the Archaic Period," *AJA* 99, no. 4 (1995): 629–30, considers Pausanias's skepticism of the ghost stories, expressed at 6.20.18 as a belief that the name Taraxippus merely referred to Poseidon, as evidence that the superstition was commonly held in ancient Greece.
48. Homer, *Iliad* 14.323–24; Hesiod, *Theogony* 315–16, 526, 530; *Homeric Hymn to Heracles* 1–2; and Herodotus 2.43–44.
49. Paus. 5.7.7–10.
50. Apollodorus, *Library* 2.5.9–12. See also Theocritus, *Idyll* 24.103–24; Paus. 3.16.4–5; Diodorus Siculus 4.23.2; and Pindar, *Isthmian* 4.52–55.

51. E.g., Homer, *Iliad* 8.362; Homer, *Odyssey* 11.622; Hesiod, *Theogony* 951; Pindar *Isthmian* 6.48; Acusilaus, frag. 29 Fowler; Apollodorus, *Library* 2.4.12; Paus. 8.18.3; and Diodorus Siculus 4.11.3.
52. Isocrates, *Helen* 17: Heracles's glory came "from wars and from *agones*."
53. Wendy J. Raschke, "Images of Victory: Some New Considerations of Athletic Monuments," in Raschke, *Archaeology of the Olympics*, 43. See also Beth Cohen, "From Bowman to Clubman: Herakles and Olympia," *Art Bulletin* 76, no. 4 (1994): 710; and Judith Barringer, "The Temple of Zeus at Olympia, Heroes, and Athletes," *Hesperia* 74 (2005): 211–41. Mark Golden, in *Sport and Society in Ancient Greece*, 146–57, presents an opposing view that contrasts Heracles's *athla* with notions of wage labor, concluding that Heracles's labors indicate the futility of working for money prizes and the value of striving for metaphysical rewards (like immortality).
54. Plutarch, *Life of Alexander* 3.
55. Demosthenes Giraud, "Leochares' Argead Portraits in the Philippeion," in *Early Hellenistic Portraiture: Image, Style, Context*, ed. Peter Schultz and Ralf Von Den Hoff (Cambridge: Cambridge University Press, 2007), 205.
56. Elizabeth D. Carney, "The Philippeum, Women, and the Formation of Dynastic Image," in *Alexander's Empire: Formulation to Decay*, ed. Waldemar Heckel, Lawrence Tritle, and Pat Wheatley (Claremont, CA: Regina Books, 2007), 36.
57. Paus. 6.11.1.

Chapter 3

1. The mythic context of this story is too complex to relate here beyond a brief summation. The seven who marched against Thebes were assembled by Polynices, one of the sons of Oedipus, as he sought to wrest the throne from his brother, Eteocles, the other son of Oedipus. The seven heroes marched to Thebes and attacked, each one assailing one of Thebes's seven gates, which were defended by seven brave Theban warriors. In the end, the defenders of Thebes warded off the attackers, but Eteocles and Polynices killed each other during the course of the battle, bringing further (but not the final) misfortunes to the house of Oedipus.
2. Simonides, *PMG* 533; Bacchylides 9.10–20; and Gantz, *Early Greek Myth*, 510–12. A scholiast's Hypothesis D to Pindar's *Nemean* odes mentions the lost play of Aeschylus. For a later version of the myth, see Apollodorus, *Library* 3.6.4. See also Stephen G. Miller, *Nemea: A Guide to the Site and Museum* (Berkeley: University of California Press, 1990), 26–27, for a synthesized summary of the myth and for a brief description of archaeological finds connected to the story.
3. Callimachus, frag. 384 Pfeiffer. Callimachus, like his Hellenistic contemporaries, often featured esoteric or obscure mythological references in his poetry as a way of "showing off" his erudition. Unfortunately, this poem has survived only in fragments.
4. Miller, *Nemea*, 2.
5. Paus. 2.15.3.
6. Strabo, *Geography* 8.6.19. The Acrocorinth is an imposing fortified mountain near Corinth.

7. Mary K. Dabney, Susan E. Allen, Anne Kugler, Anastasia Papathanasiou, and James C. Wright, "The Neolithic Settlement on Tsoungiza at Ancient Nemea," *Hesperia* 89, no. 1 (January–March 2020), 1–65.
8. Robert C. Knapp and John D. Mac Isaac, *The Coins*, vol. 3 of *Excavations at Nemea*, ed. Stephen G. Miller (Berkeley: University of California Press, 2005), 15–16.
9. Stephen G. Miller, Robert C. Knapp, and David Chamberlain, *The Early Hellenistic Stadium*, vol. 2 of *Excavations at Nemea*, ed. Stephen G. Miller (Berkeley: University of California Press, 2001), 1.
10. Jorge Bravo, *The Shrine of Opheltes*, vol. 4 of *Excavations at Nemea*, ed. Stephen G. Miller (Berkeley: University of California Press, 2018), 59.
11. Miller, Knapp, and Chamberlain, *Early Hellenistic Stadium*, 97–99; and Miller, *Nemea*, 57, 101–2.
12. Plutarch, *Life of Aratus* 28.3–4.
13. Plutarch, *Life of Aratus* 29.1–5.
14. Miller, Knapp, and Chamberlain, *Early Hellenistic Stadium*, 99, notes that, aside from this possible brief Aratus-held festival in 235 BCE, "we have no basis for believing that the Stadium at Nemea was used for athletic festivals after *ca.* 271 BCE."
15. Miller, Knapp, and Chamberlain, *Early Hellenistic Stadium*, 7–8.
16. Donald W. Bradeen, "Inscriptions from Nemea," *Hesperia* 35, no. 4 (1966): 326–29. The ending for "Nemea" is dative case and seems to be a locative in usage, indicating a place.
17. Stella G. Miller, "The Early Travelers: 1766–1883," in *The Temple of Zeus at Nemea: Perspectives and Prospects*, ed. Benaki Museum (Athens: Benaki Museum, 1983), 20.
18. Stephen G. Miller, "The Archaeologists: 1884–1979," in Benaki Museum, *Temple of Zeus at Nemea*, 40. The inscriptions are found in Georges Cousin and Félix Durrbach, "Inscriptions de Némée," *BCH* 9 (1885): 349–56.
19. Miller, "Archaeologists," 41; and René Vallois and Mogens Becker Clemmensen, "Le temple de Zeus à Némée," *BCH* 49 (1925): 1–20.
20. Bert H. Hill and Lewey T. Lands, *The Temple of Zeus at Nemea* (Princeton, NJ: American School of Classical Studies at Athens, 1966).
21. Miller, *Nemea*, 130.
22. Miller, *Nemea*, 140–41.
23. Paus. 2.20.3. Lysippos was a prominent sculptor during the fourth century BCE.
24. Hill and Lands, *Temple of Zeus at Nemea*.
25. Darice E. Birge, Lynn H. Kraynak, and Stephen G. Miller, *Topographical and Architectural Studies*, vol. 1 of *Excavations at Nemea*, ed. Stephen G. Miller (Berkeley: University of California Press, 1992), 1ff.
26. Birge, Kraynak, and Miller, *Topographical and Architectural Studies*, 6.
27. Paus. 2.15.2.
28. Pindar, *Nemean* 2.4–5; Euripides, *Hercules Furens* 359–60; and Birge, Kraynak, and Miller, *Topographical and* Architectural *Studies*, 94–95.
29. Miller, *Nemea*, 120.
30. Miller, *Nemea*, 76–77.
31. Birge, Kraynak, and Miller, *Topographical and Architectural Studies*, 102.

32. David Romano, "An Early Stadium at Nemea," *Hesperia* 46, no. 1 (1977): 27–31.
33. Birge, Kraynak, and Miller, *Topographical and Architectural Studies*, 128–30.
34. Birge, Kraynak, and Miller, *Topographical and Architectural Studies*, 173–84.
35. See Birge, Kraynak, and Miller, *Topographical and Architectural Studies*, 244–50, for discussion of the difficulties in understanding the role and function of this building. Ultimately, Miller decided to call this structure a bath, since that is "the one function which is unquestionably documented" for this structure (p. 250).
36. Paus. 2.15.3; and Hypotheses C and D to Pindar, *Nemean*.
37. Bravo, *Shrine of Opheltes*, 1–5.
38. Bravo, *Shrine of Opheltes*, 35–36.
39. Miller, *Nemea*, 26–29. For the identification of the shrine as that of Opheltes, see Bravo, *Shrine of Opheltes*, 76ff.
40. Stephen G. Miller, "The Shrine of Opheltes and the Earliest Stadium of Nemea," in Kyrieleis, *Olympia 1875–2000*, 239–50.
41. Bravo, *Shrine of Opheltes*, 77.
42. Ancient Greeks did not use numbers but used letters to indicate numerical values.
43. Miller, "Shrine of Opheltes," 247–48.
44. Miller, *Early Hellenistic Stadium*, 25–29.
45. Miller, *Early Hellenistic Stadium*, 232–37.
46. Miller, *Early Hellenistic Stadium*, 70–89, 311–66.
47. Miller, *Early Hellenistic Stadium*, 139–224.
48. Miller, *Early Hellenistic Stadium*, 93–97.

Chapter 4

1. Elizabeth R. Gebhard and Frederick P. Hemans, "University of Chicago Excavations at Isthmia, 1989: I," *Hesperia* 61, no. 1 (1992): 61.
2. Strabo, *Geography* 8.6.20.
3. Polybius, *Histories* 18.45.
4. Polybius, *Histories* 2.12.
5. Polybius, *Histories* 18.46. Of course, what Flamininus intended by using the phrase "freedom for the Greeks" and what the Greeks understood it to mean were quite different. Rome fought additional wars against the Greeks, culminating with the creation of a Roman-administered province in 146 BCE.
6. Green, *Alexander to Actium*, 448.
7. Paus. 2.2.2. For dating the return of the Isthmian Games to the Isthmian sanctuary, see Mika Kajava, "When Did the Isthmian Games Return to the Isthmus? (Rereading *Corinth* 8.3.153)," *Classical Philology* 97, no. 2 (2002): 168–78.
8. Paus. 2.1.6.
9. Apollodorus, *Library* 3.4.3; Paus. 1.44.7-8; and Hypotheses A, B, C, and D to Pindar, *Isthmian*. See Gebhard, "Beginnings of Panhellenic Games," 232, for a useful chart that compiles and compares the various mythic traditions.
10. Pindar, frag. 6.5 Snell; and Callimachus, frag. 384 Pfeiffer.
11. Oscar Broneer, "Isthmia Excavations, 1952," *Hesperia* 22, no. 3 (1953): 182–95.
12. Gebhard and Hemans, "Isthmia, 1989: I," 8.
13. Oscar Broneer, "The Isthmian Sanctuary of Poseidon," in *Neue Forschungen in*

Griechischen Heiligtümern, ed. Ulf Jantzen (Tübingen, Germany: Verlag Ernst Wasmuth, 1976), 41.

14. Broneer, "Isthmian Sanctuary," 42–43.
15. Oscar Broneer, *Temple of Poseidon*, Isthmia 1 (Princeton, NJ: American School of Classical Studies at Athens, 1971), 3. N. G. L. Hammond's suggestion in *The Cambridge Ancient History* that the Persians burned the Temple of Poseidon in 480 BCE seems unlikely. For discussion of the remains of Archaic-period armor dedications at Isthmia, see Alastar Jackson, "Arms and Armour at the Panhellenic Sanctuary of Poseidon at Isthmia," in *Proceedings of an International Symposium on the Olympic Games*, ed. William Coulson and Helmut Kyrieleis (Athens: Deutsches Archäologisches Institut, 1992), 141–44.
16. Polybius 39.17; and Paus. 2.2.2. Elizabeth Gebhard has argued that the Isthmian Games moved from Sicyon to rebuilt Corinth before returning to Isthmia in the forties CE. "The Isthmian Games and the Sanctuary of Poseidon in the Early Empire" in "The Corinthia in the Roman Period," ed. T. E. Gregory, supplement, *Journal of Roman Studies* 8, 78–94.
17. Broneer, *Temple of Poseidon*, 3.
18. Paus. 2.1.7.
19. Broneer, *Temple of Poseidon*, 1–2.
20. Broneer, *Temple of Poseidon*, 55–56; and Broneer, "Isthmian Sanctuary," 46.
21. Broneer, "Isthmian Sanctuary," 48.
22. Broneer, *Temple of Poseidon*, 103.
23. Elizabeth Gebhard, "The Early Stadium at Isthmia and the Founding of the Isthmian Games," in Coulson and Kyrieleis, *Proceedings of an International Symposium*, 75.
24. Oscar Broneer, "Excavations at Isthmia: Third Campaign, 1955–56," *Hesperia* 27, no. 1 (1958): 11–15.
25. Oscar Broneer, *Topography and Architecture*, Isthmia 2 (Princeton, NJ: American School of Classical Studies at Athens, 1973), 66.
26. Broneer, *Topography and Architecture*, 55–63.
27. Paus. 2.1.7–8.
28. Paus. 2.2.1.
29. Philostratus, *Imagines* 2.16.
30. Broneer, *Topography and Architecture*, 100–101; and Gebhard, "Early Stadium," 428–32.
31. *Topography and Architecture*, 100–101, 109n13. See Plutarch, *Life of Theseus* 25; Paus. 2.2.1; and Philostratus, *Imagines* 2.16, for ancient references to the mysteries of Palaimon.
32. "The Myth of Palaemon," *TAPA* 89 (1958): 92–98.
33. Oscar Broneer, "Excavations at Isthmia: Fourth Campaign, 1957–1958," *Hesperia* 28, no. 4 (1959): 322–23; and Broneer, "Isthmian Sanctuary," 52.
34. "Isthmian Sanctuary," 52.
35. David W. Rupp, "The Lost Classical Palaimonion Found?," *Hesperia* 48, no. 1 (1979): 64–72; and Brunilde Sismondo Ridgway, "A Poros Kouros from Isthmia," *Hesperia* 44, no. 4 (1975): 430.
36. Broneer, *Topography and Architecture*, 99–100.

37. Broneer, *Topography and Architecture*, 15; and Gebhard and Hemans, "Isthmia, 1989: I," 63–64.
38. Gebhard and Hemans, "Isthmia, 1989": I," 64.
39. Gebhard and Hemans, "Isthmia, 1989: I," 64–67.
40. Elizabeth R. Gebhard, *The Theater at Isthmia* (Chicago: University of Chicago Press, 1973).
41. Gebhard, *Theater at Isthmia*, 24–26.
42. Gebhard, *Theater at Isthmia*, 30.
43. Suetonius, *Nero* 24.
44. Paus. 2.1.7; and Gebhard, *Theater at Isthmia*, 89.
45. *IG* 2^2.3779; and Gebhard, *Theater at Isthmia*, 140.
46. Arthur Pickard-Cambridge, *The Dramatic Festivals of Athens*, 2nd ed. (Oxford: Clarendon Press, 1968), 279–305.
47. Pickard-Cambridge, *Dramatic Festivals*, 284. The inscription is published at *IG* 4.682. The number of victories at Olympia is unclear, not the reference to those victories being at Olympia.
48. Pamela M. Packard, "A Monochrome Mosaic at Isthmia," *Hesperia* 49, no. 4 (1980): 326–46.
49. Jon Frey and Timothy Gregory, "Old Excavations and New Interpretations: The 2008–2013 Seasons of The Ohio State University Excavations at Isthmia," *Hesperia* 85, no. 3 (2016): 437–90.
50. Frey and Gregory, "Old Excavations," 482–83.
51. Plutarch, *Life of Themistocles* 17.
52. Broneer, "Third Campaign," 22–23 and plate 9.
53. Paus. 2.2.1.
54. Aeschylus, *Isthmiastae* 79–90; Dana Ferrin Sutton, "Aeschylus' *Theoroi* or *Isthmiastae*: A Reconsideration," *Greek, Roman, Byzantine Studies* 22, no. 4 (1981): 337; and William Rostoker and Elizabeth Gebhard, "The Sanctuary of Poseidon at Isthmia: Techniques of Metal Manufacture," *Hesperia* 49, no. 4 (1980): 347–63.
55. Aeschylus, *Isthmiastae* 73.
56. Paus. 5.2.1–5. See also Paus. 2.15.1.
57. Plutarch, *Quaestiones Conviviales* 5.3.1.
58. Aeschylus, *Isthmiastae* 75–76. Specifically, the speaker (presumably Dionysus) chastises what seems to be the chorus of satyrs for "refusing the ivy" and wearing pine leaves instead.
59. Oscar Broneer, "The Isthmian Victory Crown," *AJA* 66, no. 3 (1962): 259–63; Pindar, *Olympian* 13.33; Pindar, *Nemean* 4.88; and Pindar, *Isthmian* 2.16, 8.64.
60. Dio Chrysostom 37.14–15; and Borimir Jordan, "Isthmian Amusements," *Classics Ireland* 8 (2001): 38.
61. Dio Chrysostom 8.5ff.
62. Dio Chrysostom 9.5–18.
63. Oscar Broneer, "The Apostle Paul and the Isthmian Games," *Biblical Archaeologist* 25, no. 1 (1962): 1–31.
64. David R. Jordan, "Inscribed Lead Tablets from the Games in the Sanctuary of Poseidon," *Hesperia* 63, no. 1 (1994): 111–26.

65. Daniel J. Geagan, "The Isthmian Dossier of P. Licinius Priscus Juventianus," *Hesperia* 58, no. 3 (1989): 349–60. There were actually two inscriptions connected to Priscus's contributions to Isthmia, and Geagan argues convincingly that these were in fact portions of the same original. The inscription discovered first (in the seventeenth century and taken to Italy) is published at *IG* 4.203. The second inscription was unearthed in the 1930s and published by Oscar Broneer in "An Official Rescript from Corinth," *Hesperia* 8 (1939): 181–90.
66. Plutarch, *Quaestiones Conviviales* 675B.

Chapter 5

1. Frederik Poulsen, *Delphi*, trans. G. C. Richards (London: Gylendal, 1920), 38.
2. Strabo 9.3.6. Strabo credits Pindar with this story, which presumably appeared in a poem that is no longer extant.
3. Strabo 9.3.4.
4. There are occasional attempts to fix the transition of the Pythian festival to Panhellenic Crown Games status in 586 BCE, based on the first part of a passage in Pausanias. Pausanias explains that the site had featured musical competitions for many years, and Paus. 10.7.4–5 indicates that in the third year of the forty-eighth Olympiad (ancient Greeks counted inclusively, so this equates to 586 BCE, two years after the Olympian festival of 588), the organizers augmented the music competitions and offered prizes for athletes. This would be the beginning of the Pythian Games including nonmusical competitions but not their being Crown Games, since the officials awarded prizes. According to Pausanias, at the *second* Pythian festival to include athletic events (i.e., in 582), the organizers discontinued prizes and offered crowns instead. The institution of crown-giving marks the transition of the Pythian festival to *stephanitic* (i.e., crown-giving) status and part of the Crown Games circuit.
5. *Homeric Hymn to Apollo* 357.
6. *Homeric Hymn to Apollo* 363.
7. See also Euripides's play *Iphigenia in Tauris* 1234–57 for an account of the mythic beginnings of Apollo's sanctuary and oracle at Delphi.
8. Hyginus, *Fabula* 140. See also Apollodorus, *Library* 1.4.1.
9. Poulsen, *Delphi*, 44.
10. Poulsen, *Delphi*, 44–46.
11. Poulsen, *Delphi*, 46; and Théophile Homolle, "Institut de correspondance hellenique," *BCH* 17 (1893): 185.
12. Paus. 10.5.3; Peter Levi's translation from Pausanias, *Guide to Greece*, trans. Peter Levi, vol. 1, *Central Greece* (London: Penguin Press, 1971), 415.
13. Paus. 10.8.5.
14. Jean Jannoray, *Le gymnase*, fasc. 12 of *Topographie et architecture*, *FD* 2 (Paris: Éditions de Boccard, 1953), 4.
15. Théophile Homolle, "Communication: Le gymnase de Delphes," *BCH* 23 (1899): 563–656.
16. Jannoray, *Le gymnase*, 85.
17. Pierre Amandry, "La fête des Pythia," *Pratika tes Akademias Athenon* 65 (1990): 295.

18. For the sanctuary of Demeter, see Jannoray, *Le gymnase* 21ff. For the two heroes, see Herodotus 8.39.1.
19. Pouilloux, "Travaux à Delphes," 103–23.
20. Vitruvius, *On Architecture* 5.11; and Olga Tzachou-Alexandri, "The Gymnasium: An Institution for Athletics and Education," in *Mind and Body: Athletic Contests in Ancient Greece* (Athens: Ministry of Culture, 1989), 34.
21. Paus. 10.8.5.
22. Michael Scott, *Delphi and Olympia* (Cambridge: Cambridge University Press, 2010), 35, 51–53.
23. Paus. 10.9.1ff.
24. See École française d'Athènes, *Inscriptions de l'entrée du sanctuaire au trésor des Athéniens*, fasc. 1 of *Épigraphie*, *FD* 3, 27. The first epigram commends both the individual glory of Lysander and the victory of Sparta in the Peloponnesian War that ended in 404 BCE.
25. Herodotus 3.57; and Paus. 10.11.2.
26. For the ancient sources, see Apollodorus, *Library* 2.4.2; Plutarch, *Moralia* 557d; and Paus. 8.15.5. H. W. Parke and John Boardman, "The Struggle for the Tripod and the First Sacred War," *JHS* 77, part 2 (1957): 276–82, suggests that the struggle for the tripod symbolized the struggle of the Delphic Amphictyons against the community of Kirrha during the First Sacred War of the early sixth century BCE.
27. Paus. 10.11.4.
28. Scott, *Delphi and Olympia*, 112–13; and Poulsen, *Delphi*, 168–97.
29. Poulsen, *Delphi*, 164–65; and Gaston Colin, "Le culte d'Apollon Pythien à Athènes au IVe siècle au IIe," *BCH* 20 (1896): 639–41. Plutarch, *Life of Aristides* 20.4, relates that, after the Battle of Plataea in 479 BCE, the Greeks in the area extinguished all fires and rekindled them with fire from Delphi.
30. The hymns are published in Annie Bélis, *Les hymnes à Apollon*, vol. 3 of *CID* (Paris: Éditions de Boccard, 1992).
31. For an English translation of these paeans, see Thomas J. Mathiesen, *Apollo's Lyre: Greek Music and Music Theory in Antiquity and the Middle Ages* (Lincoln: University of Nebraska Press, 1999), 42–43.
32. Paus. 10.5.9–13. See also Christiane Sourvinou-Inwood, "The Myth of the First Temples at Delphi," *Classical Quarterly* 29, no. 12 (1979): 231–51.
33. Herodotus 5.62–63.
34. See Paus. 10.19.4.
35. Plato, *Charmides* 165A.
36. Strabo 9.3.6.
37. Homer, *Odyssey* 8.80.
38. Herodotus 7.220.
39. Herodotus 7.141.
40. Plutarch, *Life of Alexander* 14.4.
41. Plato, *Apology* 21A.
42. Livy 5.16.8–11; and Plutarch, *Life of Cicero* 5.1.
43. Joseph Fontenrose, *The Delphic Oracle* (Berkeley: University of California Press, 1978), oracle Q243 (Parke and Wormell 476). Fontenrose dismisses this oracle as "quasi-historical" (hence the *Q* in his assigned number). See Timothy

Gregory, "Julian and the Last Oracle at Delphi," *Greek, Roman, Byzantine Studies* 24 (1983): 355–66, for a discussion of the oracle's possible fourth-century-CE provenance and its role in Christianizing the Roman Empire in Greece.

44. Paus. 10.7.2–3.
45. Amandry, "La fête des Pythia," 307. The principal surviving example of dating in this way is a third-century-BCE inscription from Magnesia (*SIG* 557).
46. *Ancient Greek Music* (Oxford: Clarendon Press, 1992), 1.
47. West, *Ancient Greek Music*, 106; and Plutarch, *Life of Alcibiades* 2.5.
48. Plutarch, *On Music* 1134A; and Paus. 2.22.8, 10.7.4
49. Paus. 10.7.7.
50. Pollux 4.66, cited in West, *Ancient Greek Music*, 59.
51. Mathiesen, *Apollo's Lyre*, 60–61.
52. Paus. 3.12.10.
53. Plato, *Republic* 4.424B.
54. Strabo 9.3.10. Strabo tells us that the last section of the performance imitated the dragon's last breaths.
55. Amandry, "La fête des Pythia," 307.
56. Paus. 10.7.5.
57. Mathiesen, *Apollo's Lyre*, 44.
58. Orsamus Pearl, "Rules for Musical Contests," *Illinois Classical Studies* 3 (1978): 132–39.
59. Didier Laroche, *Sujet: Sanctuaire d'Apollon et stade* [Subject: Sanctuary of Apollo and stadium], 1988, drawing, École français d'Athènes, https://archimage.efa.gr/?kroute=fiche_publique&id=514442.
60. M. Perdrizet, "Les bas-reliefs du théâtre de Delphes," *BCH* 21 (1897): 600–603.
61. Apollodorus, *Epitome* 5.21; and Paus. 10.27.2.
62. Euripides, *Andromache* 49–55, 1086–165. Joseph Fontenrose, *The Cult and Myth of Pyrros at Delphi* (Berkeley: University of California Press, 1960), 212–13, identified five different versions of this myth and some conflations of these versions. In myth, the god Apollo helped the Trojan prince Paris kill Achilles by shooting him in his vulnerable spot at the back of his heel.
63. Paus. 4.17.4.
64. Pindar, *Nemean* 7.34–42.
65. Paus. 10.24.4–6.
66. Paus. 10.26.4.
67. Paus. 1.4.4 asserts that the hero Neoptolemus appeared to repel the Gauls from Delphi in 279/8 BCE, leading the people of Delphi to sacrifice to him as a hero, having previously held his tomb in contempt. Although the ode discussed here is a *Nemean* ode, Pindar's retelling of the Neoptolemus story takes his audience to Delphi. See Pindar *Nemean* 7.44–47 for Neoptolemus's overseeing the rituals at Delphi.
68. Apollodorus, *Epitome* 6.14; Strabo 9.3.9; Paus. 4.17.4, 10.7.1; Hyginus, *Fabula* 123; Pindar, *Nemean* 7.34.42; and Pherecydes, frag. 64 Fowler.
69. Jean Pouilloux, *La région nord du sanctuaire (de l'époque archaïque à la fin du sanctuaire)*, fasc. 13 of *Topographie et architecture*, *FD* 2 (Paris: École française d'Athènes, 1960), 51–53.
70. Pouilloux, *La région nord*, 57.

71. Pouilloux, *La région nord*, 57, indicated that the excavations offered "more mysteries" ("*plus d'énigmes*") than answers about Neoptolemus at Delphi.
72. Pouilloux, *La région nord*, 58–59. See Paus. 1.11.2 for Pergamos.
73. Pindar, *Nemean* 7.45–46.
74. Paus. 10.32.1.
75. Pindar, *Pythian* 10.15–16, 11.13.
76. Théophile Homolle, "Topographie de Delphes," *BCH* 21(1897): 269–270, plates 14–15.
77. Théophile Homolle, "Le stade de Delphes," *BCH* 23 (1899): 609.
78. Paus. 10.32.1.
79. Pierre Aupert, *Le stade*. fasc. 9 of *Topographie et architecture*, Fouilles des Delphes 2 (Paris: Éditions de Boccard, 1979), 68.
80. Georges Rougemont, *Lois sacrées et règlements religieux*, vol. 1 of *CID* (Paris: Éditions de Boccard, 1977), no. 3. For commentary on the inscription's difficulties, see P. Fournier, "L'inscription du stade de delphes," *Révue des études anciennes* (1922): 5–12; and Georges Rougemont and Denis Rousset, *Nouveau choix d'inscriptions grecques* (Paris: Les Belles Lettres, 1971), no. 18.
81. In essence, the discussion boils down to the difference between the words (transliterated) *es* and *eis*. Variations in ancient Greek dialects and damage to this word on the stone make a definitive reading difficult.
82. Homolle, "Le stade de Delphes," 611–12.
83. See, e.g., Allen Guttmann, *Sports Spectators* (New York: Columbia University Press, 1986), 17.
84. Homolle, "Le stade de Delphes," 611–12. See also Rougemont's commentary in *Lois sacrées et règlements religieux*, pp. 12–13.
85. Aupert, *Le stade*.
86. Aupert, *Le stade*, 40.

Chapter 6

1. Paus. 6.1.1–2.
2. Diodorus Siculus 12.9.5–6; Paus. 6.14.5–9; and Strabo 6.1.12.
3. For general discussion of Milo and the other "heroic athletes," see David J. Lunt, "The Heroic Athlete in Ancient Greece," *Journal of Sport History* 36, no. 3 (2009): 375–92; and Bruno Currie, *Pindar and the Cult of Heroes* (Oxford: Oxford University Press), 120–57.
4. Xenophon, *On Hunting* 1.17.
5. Plutarch, *Life of Theseus* 35; and Herodotus 8.64, 83–84. Peleus was the father of Achilles and Telamon the father of Ajax.
6. Plutarch, *Life of Lysander* 12.
7. Paus. 4.32.4–6.
8. Diodorus Siculus 9.14.2. See Paus. 6.5.1, 4–9 for Polydamas's exploits.
9. Anna Maranti, *Olympia & Olympic Games* (Athens: Toubis, 1999), 102–3.
10. See Lucian, *Parliament of the Gods* 12, for the healing power of the statue.
11. Paus. 6.8.5; and Philostratus, *Gymnasticus* 22.
12. Paus. 7.27.2.
13. Athenaeus 10.412 D–F; Dio Chrysostom 31.95–97; Lucian, *Parliament of the*

Gods 12; Paus. 6.6.5–6, 6.11.2–9; and Plutarch, *Moralia* 811D–E. His name is sometimes spelled Theogenes.

14. Paus. 6.11.5.
15. See Susan C. Jones, "Statues That Kill and the Gods Who Love Them," in *ΣΤΕΦΑΝΟΣ: Studies in Honor of Brunilde Sismondo Ridgway*, ed. Kim J. Hartswick and Mary C. Sturgeon (Philadelphia: University Museum, University of Pennsylvania, 1998), 139–43, for a discussion of this episode.
16. Jean Pouilloux, *Récherches sur l'histoire et les cultes de Thasos*, vol. 1 (Paris: École française d'Athènes, 1954), 102–3, dates Theagenes and his cult according to Thásos's relationship with Persia, Athens, and Athenian law during the fifth century BCE, as demonstrated through the details of the statue's "trial."
17. Paus. 6.11.9.
18. The discovery of the treasury and its inscriptions were first published in R. Martin, "Un Nouveau Règlement De Culte Thasien," *BCH* 64–65 (1940–41): 163–200.
19. *SIG* 36; and *IAG* 21. The inscription goes on to mention Theagenes's Olympian, Pythian, Isthmian, and Nemean victories, as well as a victory in the *dolichos* running race at Argos. For commentary, see Desmond Schmidt, "An Unusual Victory List from Keos: *IG* XII, 5, 608 and the Dating of Bakchylides," *JHS* 119 (1999): 76–77; and Elizabeth Pierce Blegen, "Archaeological News," *AJA* 53, no. 4 (1949): 368. See Pouilloux, *Récherches sur l'histoire*, 78–82, for comparisons between the versions of this inscription found at Olympia, Delphi, and Thásos, as well as for a summary of proposed reconstructions for the first two lines.
20. Paus. 6.11.9.
21. Paus. 6.6.6.
22. Paus. 6.6.7–11; and Bruno Currie, "Euthymos of Locri: A Case Study in Heroization in the Classical Period," *JHS* 122 (2002): 24–44.
23. Paus. 6.8.3; Diodorus Siculus 13.68; and Xenophon, *Hellenica* 1.2.1.
24. *IAG* 464.
25. Athenaeus 4.135D, 10.413B.
26. Paus. 8.40.1–2.
27. Philostratus, *Gymnasticus* 21; and *Imagines* 2.6.
28. In Greek myth, the jealous Zephyr caused Apollo's discus to swerve and kill young Hyacinth. Apollodorus, *Library* 1.3.3; and Ovid, *Metamorphoses* 10.162–219. Perseus accidentally killed his grandfather Akrisios with an errant discus throw that struck the old man's foot. Apollodorus, *Library* 2.4.4; and Paus. 2.16.2. Pausanias 5.3.7 reports that Oxylos, the mythic founder of Elis, went into exile after an errant discus throw killed a bystander. There is also the myth where Telamon and Peleus killed their brother deliberately with a discus, for which the two went into exile.
29. Demosthenes 23 (*Against Aristocrates* 53); Plato, *Laws* 9.865A–B; and David J. Lunt, "Sanctioned Violence: Dealing (with) Death in Ancient Greek Athletics," *Journal of Olympic Studies* 1, no. 2 (Fall 2020): 32–47.
30. Paus. 8.40.3–5. For Creugas's statue, see Paus. 2.20.1. Pausanias's comment about how the competitors did not yet employ heavy wrappings on their arms places this fight before 400 BCE. R. H. Brophy, "Deaths in the Pan-Hellenic

Games: Arrachion and Creugas," *American Journal of Philology*, 99, no. 3 (Autumn 1978): 382.

31. Paus. 6.9.6–8; and Plutarch, *Life of Romulus* 28.
32. Paus. 6.9.8.
33. Plutarch, *Life of Aratus* 3; and Pausanias 6.12.5–6.
34. Plutarch, *Life of Aratus* 28.3–4.
35. Pindar, *Isthmian* 4.45–48.
36. Paus. 7.27.2; and Athenaeus 11.509B.
37. *IAG* 15. The last line, referring to the number of Callias's victories in the Athenian Panathenaea, merely says *megala* (a great number).
38. Paus. 5.9.3., 6.6.1. Callias's statue base at Olympia has been unearthed. It states: "Callias the Athenian, son of Didymias. Mikon the Athenian made [the statue]." *IAG* 15.
39. Prominent Athenian politicians could be exiled or ostracized for ten years if public opinion was strong enough. The process required citizens to scratch onto broken pottery pieces (ostraca) the name of the person they wanted ostracized, and then the results would be tallied by city officials. Since typically only the most prominent Athenian politicians risked ostracism, there was a perverse honor in being considered. Eugene Vanderpool, "Some Ostraka from the Athenian Agora," *Hesperia Supplements* 8 (1949): 409–10.
40. Paus. 6.4.6–7.
41. Pindar, *Olympian* 7.15.
42. Paus. 6.7.1, 6.7.4–7.
43. Plutarch, *Life of Pelopidas* 34.4.
44. Thucydides 3.8, 8.35; and Xenophon, *Hellenica* 1.1.2.
45. Xenophon, *Hellenica* 1.5.19; and Paus. 6.7.5. Later in the war, when Rhodes left the Spartan alliance and joined with Athens again, Dorieus happened to be in Spartan-controlled territory. Unfortunately, the great athlete was quickly captured by Spartans and executed. Paus. 6.7.6.
46. Paus. 5.6.7–8; and Philostratus, *Gymnasticus* 17.
47. Paus. 6.20.9.
48. Matthew Dillon, "Did Parthenoi Attend the Olympic Games? Girls and Women Competing, Spectating, and Carrying out Cult Roles at Greek Religious Festivals," *Hermes* 128, no. 4 (2000): 457–60.
49. *IAG* 17; Donald G. Kyle, "'The Only Woman in All Greece': Kyniska, Agesilaus, Alcibiades and Olympia," *Journal of Sport History* 30, no. 2 (2003): 183–203; and Paus. 5.12.5, 6.1.6.
50. Paus. 3.8.1.
51. Paus. 5.8.11.
52. Golden, *Sport and Society*, 87. Callimachus's poem is called (today) "Victoria Berenices" and survives only in fragments.
53. École française d'Athènes, *Inscriptions de l'entrée*, 534; *SIG* 802; and *IAG* 63.
54. Paus. 10.4.2.
55. Although the term "tyrant" (*tyrannos*) had acquired its negative connotation at the time of the earliest literature of ancient Greece and especially in Athens (as something opposed to democratic rule), the term itself sometimes carried

no stigma, and occasionally the word was used as a compliment to a strong and capable ruler. See A. Andrewes, *The Greek Tyrants* (New York: Harper and Row, 1962), 20–30.

56. Herodotus 6.103. See Kurke, *Traffic in Praise*, 179–80, for analysis of this episode.
57. Plutarch, *Life of Lysander* 18. Plutarch, *Life of Alcibiades* 7, relates that the philosopher Socrates gave his prize for valor at Potidaea to Alcibiades.
58. David Lunt, "The Thrill of Victory and the Avoidance of Defeat: Alexander as a Sponsor of Athletic Contests," *Ancient History Bulletin* 28, no. 3–4 (2014): 119–34.
59. Thucydides 6.16.1, 6.15.4.
60. Xenophon, *Hellenica* 4.5.1–2; and Plutarch, *Life of Agesilaus* 21.
61. Plutarch, *Life of Agesilaus* 21.
62. Xenophon, *Hellenica* 6.4.29-32.
63. Diodorus Siculus 16.60.2.
64. Plutarch, *Life of Demetrius* 40.
65. Timothy Howe, "Kings Don't Lie: Truthtelling, Historiography and Ptolemy I Soter," in *Ptolemy I Soter: A Self-Made Man*, ed. Timothy Howe (Oxford: Oxbow Books, 2018), 175–77.
66. Paus. 10.7.8. See Sofie Remijsen, "Challenged by Egyptians: Greek Sports in the Third Century," in *Sport in the Cultures of the Ancient World*, ed. Zinon Papakonstantinou (New York: Routledge, 2010), 116n16, for the date of 314 BCE.
67. Howe, "Kings Don't Lie," 175–77.
68. The Posidippus epigrams are published in C. Austin and G. Bastianini, eds. *Posidippi Pellaei quae supersunt omia* (Milan: LED), 2002. The surviving poems of Posidippus, including an English translation of the *Hippika* epigrams, are available from the electronic journal *Classics@*, vol. 1 (first published in 2002 and last updated in February 2021), published by the Center for Hellenic Studies at Harvard University, available at http://nrs.harvard.edu/urn-3:hlnc.jissue:ClassicsAt.Issue01.New_Epigrams_Attributed_to_Possidippus.2002-. See also Remijsen, "Challenged by Egyptians," 98–124.
69. Posidippus 79.
70. Posidippus 78. See Remijsen, "Challenged by Egyptians," 103–6, for commentary on the term *aethlophorous*.
71. Posidippus 87. The epigram uses the word *kudos* rather than *kleos*. Although both words translate roughly to "glory," the term *kudos* seems to have possessed more mystical connotations. See Kurke, "Economy of Kudos," 132; and Lunt, "Heroic Athlete," 377–78.
72. "Kings Don't Lie," 176.
73. Paus. 6.3.11–12.
74. For Hiero's dedications at Olympia, see Paus. 6.12.1, 8.42.8–10.
75. Théophile Homolle, "Statue de bronze découverte à Delphes, séance du 5 juin 1896, appendice," *Comptes rendus des séances de l'Académie des Inscriptions et Belles-Lettres* 40, no. 4 (1896): 362–84.
76. Diodorus Siculus 14.109.
77. Paus. 6.2.6.

Chapter 7

1. Herodotus 2.160.1–4. See also Diodorus Siculus 1.95.
2. Paus. 6.3.7, 8.45.4; and Diodorus Siculus 14.54.
3. Xenophon, *Hellenica* 7.4.12.
4. Xenophon, *Hellenica* 7.4.14.
5. Xenophon, *Hellenica* 7.4.28–32. Diodorus Siculus 15.78.1–3 records a slightly garbled version of this battle, indicating that the Eleans were holding the games when the Pisans showed up to oppose them. Diodorus agrees with Xenophon that a memorable battle took place (he calls it "strongly contested"—*kartera*) and that the Greeks attending the Olympian festival calmly applauded feats of valor on both sides.
6. E.g., Kyle, *Sport and Spectacle*, 112, notes that "except for the equestrian events, almost all contests took place in the stadium" at Olympia. Ludwig Drees, *Olympia: Gods, Artists, and Athletes*, trans. Gerald Onn (New York: Praeger, 1968), 87, says: "The athletic events were held in the stadium and the equestrian events in the hippodrome."
7. Xenophon, *Anabasis* 4.3.7–11.
8. Xenophon, *Hellenica* 7.4.31.
9. Mika Kajava, "Hestia: Hearth, Goddess, and Cult," *Harvard Studies in Classical Philology* 102 (2004): 1–2.
10. Stephen G. Miller, *The Prytaneion: Its Function and Architectural Form* (Berkeley: University of California Press, 1978), 13.
11. Paus. 5.14.4.
12. Miller, *Prytaneion*, 90, 235–39.
13. Pickard-Cambridge, *Dramatic Festivals*, 279ff.
14. Plutarch, *Life of Aratus* 28.3–4.
15. *IG* IV.682.
16. Philostratus, *Apollonius of Tyana* 6.10.2.
17. Lucian, *Herodotus*, passim but especially 2 and 7.
18. Very little of Gorgias's oration and only a portion of Lysias's have survived. Isocrates's "Panegyricus" speech was written to be delivered at Olympia.
19. Diodorus Siculus 14.109.
20. Lucian, *The Passing of Peregrinus* 21. Lucian laughed because Peregrinus seemed to have anticipated that the crowd would implore him not to jump into the fire. Instead, the crowd urged poor Peregrinus to end his own life.
21. Judith Barringer, "The Olympic Altis Before the Temple of Zeus," *Jahrbuch des Deutschen Archäologischen Institutes* 124 (2009): 223–50.
22. Paus. 10.9.1.
23. Xenophon's description of the battle includes combatants atop the Altis's buildings. *Hellenica* 7.4.31–32. Coupled with this, the fact that this is the only recorded battle that actually took place within the Altis makes it seems clear that the battle between the Eleans and the Arcadians in 364 BCE is overwhelmingly the best candidate for the moment of this soldier's death.
24. Paus. 5.20.4–5. See Miller, *Arete*, 188, for the dating of the discovery.
25. Information about past and future New Nemean Games can be found at https://nemeangames.org.

SELECTED BIBLIOGRAPHY

The scholarship associated with the sites and festivals of the Crown Games is vast and spans multiple disciplines. Therefore, the following list of modern sources is not a comprehensive treatment. Rather, it is intended to provide a general basis for and introduction to this book's sites, themes, and topics.

Ancient Greek Athletes, Contests, and Festivals

Burkert, Walter. *Greek Religion.* Translated by John Raffan. Cambridge, MA: Harvard University Press, 1985.

Cebrián, Reyes Bertolín. *The Athlete in the Ancient Greek World.* Norman: University of Oklahoma Press, 2020.

Christesen, Paul, and Donald G. Kyle, eds. *A Companion to Sport and Spectacle in Greek and Roman Antiquity.* Malden, MA: Wiley-Blackwell, 2014.

Crowther, Nigel. *Sport in Ancient Times.* Westport, CT: Praeger, 2007.

Dillon, Matthew. "Did Parthenoi Attend the Olympic Games? Girls and Women Competing, Spectating, and Carrying out Cult Roles at Greek Religious Festivals." *Hermes* 128, no. 4 (2000): 457–80.

Finley, M. I., and H. W. Pleket. *The Olympic Games: The First Thousand Years.* London: Chatto & Windus, 1976.

Golden, Mark. *Sport and Society in Ancient Greece.* Cambridge: Cambridge University Press, 1998.

Kurke, Leslie. *The Traffic in Praise: Pindar and the Poetics of Social Economy.* Ithaca, NY: Cornell University Press, 1991.

Kyle, Donald G. "'The Only Woman in All Greece': Kyniska, Agesilaus, Alcibiades and Olympia." *Journal of Sport History* 30, no. 2 (2003): 183–203.

Kyle, Donald G. *Sport and Spectacle in the Ancient World.* 2nd ed. Malden, MA: Wiley-Blackwell, 2015.

Lämmer, Manfred. "The So-Called Olympic Peace in Ancient Greece." In *Greek Athletics*, edited by Jason König, 36–60. Edinburgh: Edinburgh University Press, 2010.

Lunt, David J. "The Heroic Athlete in Ancient Greece." *Journal of Sport History* 36, no. 3 (2009): 375–92.

Mikalson, Jon D. *Ancient Greek Religion.* 2nd ed. Malden, MA: Wiley-Blackwell, 2009.

Miller, Stephen G. *Ancient Greek Athletics.* New Haven, CT: Yale University Press, 2004.

Moretti, Jean-Charles, and Panos Valvanis, eds. "Les hippodromes et les concours hippiques dans la Grèce antique." Supplement, *Bulletin de correspondance hellénique* 62 (2019).

Moretti, Luigi. *Iscrizioni agonistiche greche.* Rome: A. Signorelli, 1953.

Nicholson, Nigel. *Aristocracy and Athletics in Archaic and Classical Greece.* Cambridge: Cambridge University Press, 2005.

Nielsen, Thomas Heine. *Two Studies in the History of Ancient Greek Athletics.* Copenhagen: Royal Danish Academy of Sciences and Letters, 2018.

Pearl, Orsamus. "Rules for Musical Contests." *Illinois Classical Studies* 3 (1978): 132–39.

Poliakoff, Michael B. *Combat Sports in the Ancient World.* New Haven, CT: Yale University Press, 1987.

Potter, David. *The Victor's Crown.* Oxford: Oxford University Press, 2012.

Sansone, David. *Greek Athletics and the Genesis of Sport.* Berkeley: University of California Press, 1998.

Scanlon, Thomas. *Eros and Greek Athletics.* Oxford: Oxford University Press, 2002.

Young, David. *The Olympic Myth of Greek Amateur Athletics.* Chicago: Ares Publishers, 1985.

Olympia

Barringer, Judith M. "The Temple of Zeus at Olympia, Heroes, and Athletes." *Hesperia* 74 (2005): 211–41.

Christesen, Paul. "Whence 776? The Origin of the Date for the First Olympiad." In *Sport in the Cultures of the Ancient World: New Perspectives*, edited by Zinon Papakonstantinou, 13–34. London: Routledge, 2010.

Davidson, John. "Olympia and the Chariot-Race of Pelops." In Phillips and Pritchard, *Sport and Festival*, 101–22.

Dittenberger, Wilhelm, and Karl Purgold, eds. *Die Inschriften von Olympia.* Berlin: Asher, 1896.

Dörpfeld, Wilhelm. *Alt-Olympia.* 2 vols. Berlin: Verlag von E. S. Mittler & Sohn, 1935.

Drees, Ludwig. *Olympia: Gods, Artists, and Athletes.* Translated by Gerald Onn. New York: Praeger, 1968.

Gardiner, E. Norman. *History and Remains of Olympia.* Oxford: Oxford University Press, 1925.

Kyrieleis, Helmut. *Anfänge und Frühzeit des Heiligtums von Olympia: Die Ausgrabungen am Pelopion 1987–1996.* Olympische Forschungen 31. Berlin: Walter de Gruyter, 2006.

Kyrieleis, Helmut. "The German Excavations at Olympia: An Introduction." In Phillips and Pritchard, *Sport and Festival*, 41–60.

Mallwitz, Alfred. "Cult and Competition Locations at Olympia." In *The Archaeology of the Olympics: The Olympics and Other Festivals in Antiquity*, edited by Wendy J. Raschke, 79–109. Madison: University of Wisconsin Press, 1988.

Mallwitz, Alfred. *Olympia und seine Bauten.* Munich: Prestel-Verlag, 1972.

Miller, Stephen G. "The Organization and Functioning of the Olympic Games." In Phillips and Pritchard, *Sport and Festival*, 1–40.

Phillips, David, and David Pritchard, eds. *Sport and Festival in the Ancient Greek World.* Swansea: Classical Press of Wales, 2003.

Picard, Charles. "Les fouilles allemandes au Stade d'Olympie et l'histoire des jeux sacrés." *Revue archéologique* 1 (1961): 217–21.

Siewert, Peter, and Hans Taeuber. *Neue Inschriften von Olympia: Die ab 1896 veroffentlichten Texte*. Vienna: Verlag Holzhausen, 2013.

Spivey, Nigel. *The Ancient Olympics: A History*. Oxford: Oxford University Press, 2004.

Swaddling, Judith. *The Ancient Olympic Games*. 3rd ed. Austin: University of Texas Press, 2015.

Nemea

Benaki Museum. *The Temple of Zeus at Nemea: Perspectives and Prospects*. Athens: Benaki Museum, 1983. Exhibition brochure.

Birge, Darice E., Lynn H. Kraynak, and Stephen G. Miller. *Topographical and Architectural Studies*. Vol. 1 of *Excavations at Nemea*, edited by Stephen G. Miller. Berkeley: University of California Press, 1992.

Blegen, Carl W. "Excavations at Nemea 1926." *American Journal of Archaeology* 31, no. 4 (1927): 421–40.

Bravo, Jorge. *The Shrine of Opheltes*. Vol. 4 of *Excavations at Nemea*, edited by Stephen G. Miller. Berkeley: University of California Press, 2018.

Hill, Bert H., and Lewey T. Lands. *The Temple of Zeus at Nemea*. Princeton, NJ: American School of Classical Studies at Athens, 1966.

Knapp, Robert C., and John D. Mac Isaac. *The Coins*. Vol. 3 of *Excavations at Nemea*, edited by Stephen G. Miller. Berkeley: University of California Press, 2005.

Miller, Stephen G. *Nemea: A Guide to the Site and Museum*. Berkeley: University of California Press, 1990.

Miller, Stephen G. "The Shrine of Opheltes and the Earliest Stadium of Nemea." In *Olympia 1875–2000: 125 Jahre deutsche Ausgrabungen*, edited by Helmut Kyrieleis, 329–250. Mainz: Verlag Philipp von Zabern, 2002.

Miller, Stephen G., Robert C. Knapp, and David Chamberlain. *The Early Hellenistic Stadium*. Vol. 2 of *Excavations at Nemea*, edited by Stephen G. Miller. Berkeley: University of California Press, 2001.

Isthmia

Broneer, Oscar. "The Isthmian Victory Crown," *American Journal of Archaeology*, vol. 66, no. 3 (1962): 259–63.

Broneer, Oscar. *Temple of Poseidon*. Isthmia 1. Princeton, NJ: American School of Classical Studies at Athens, 1971.

Broneer, Oscar. *Topography and Architecture*. Isthmia 2. Princeton, NJ: American School of Classical Studies at Athens, 1973.

Frey, Jon, and Timothy Gregory. "Old Excavations and New Interpretations: The 2008–2013 Seasons of The Ohio State University Excavations at Isthmia." *Hesperia* 85, no. 3 (2016): 437–90.

Gebhard, Elizabeth R. "The Beginnings of Panhellenic Games at the Isthmus." In *Olympia 1875–2000: 125 Jahre deutsche Ausgrabungen*, edited by Helmut Kyrieleis, 221–37. Mainz: Philipp von Zabern, 2002.

Gebhard, Elizabeth R. "The Early Stadium at Isthmia and the Founding of the Isthmian Games." In *Proceedings of an International Symposium on the Olympic*

Games, edited by William Coulson and Helmut Kyrieleis, 73–79. Athens: Deutsches Archäologisches Institut, 1992.
Gebhard, Elizabeth R. *The Theater at Isthmia*. Chicago: University of Chicago Press, 1973.
Gebhard, Elizabeth R., and Matthew W. Dickie. "Melikertes-Palaimon, Hero of the Isthmian Games." In *Ancient Greek Hero Cult*, edited by Robin Hägg, 159–65. Stockholm: Paul Aströms Förlag, 1999.
Gebhard, Elizabeth R., and Frederick P. Hemans. "University of Chicago Excavations at Isthmia, 1989: I." *Hesperia* 61, no. 1 (1992): 1–77.
Hawthorne, John G. "The Myth of Palaemon." *Transactions of the American Philological Association* 89 (1958): 92–98.
Jordan, Borimir. "Isthmian Amusements." *Classics Ireland* 8 (2001): 32–67.
Kajava, Mika. "When Did the Isthmian Games Return to the Isthmus? (Rereading *Corinth* 8.3.153)." *Classical* Philology 97, no. 2 (2002): 168–78.
Rupp, David W. "The Lost Classical Palaimonion Found?" *Hesperia* 48, no. 1 (1979): 64–72.

Delphi

Amandry, Pierre. "La fête des Pythia." *Pratika tes Akademias Athenon* 65 (1990): 279–317.
Bommelaer, Jean-François. *Guide de Delphes: Le Site*. 2nd ed. Athens: École française d'Athènes, 2015.
École français d'Athènes. *Corpus des inscriptions de Delphes*. 4 vols. Athens: École française d'Athènes, 1977–2002.
École français d'Athènes. *Fouilles de Delphes*. 5 vols. Athens: École française d'Athènes, 1902–2019.
Fontenrose, Joseph. *The Cult and Myth of Pyrros at Delphi*. Berkeley: University of California Press, 1960.
Fontenrose, Joseph. "The Cult of Apollo and the Games at Delphi." In *The Archaeology of the Olympics*, edited by Wendy J. Raschke, 121–39. Madison: University of Wisconsin Press, 1988.
Fontenrose, Joseph. *The Delphic Oracle*. Berkeley: University of California Press, 1978.
Pouilloux, Jean. "Travaux à Delphes à l'occasion des Pythia." In "Études delphiques." Supplement, *Bulletin de correspondance hellénique* 4 (1977): 103–23.
Poulson, Frederik. *Delphi*. Translated by G. C. Richards. London: Gylendal, 1920.
Scott, Michael. *Delphi: A History of the Center of the Ancient World*. Princeton, NJ: Princeton University Press, 2014.

INDEX

Note: "Games," when capitalized, refers to the Crown Games only; page numbers set in italics refer to illustrations.